I0845775

UNINVITED

TRUE EXTRATERRESTRIAL ENCOUNTERS

GEMMA JADE

BEYOND
THE FRAY PUBLISHING

Copyright © 2026 by Gemma Jade
Published by: Beyond The Fray Publishing

This book or any portion thereof may not be reproduced or used in any manner whatsoever without the express written permission of the publisher except for the use of brief quotations in a book review. All rights reserved.

ISBN 13: 979-8-89234-148-6

Beyond The Fray Publishing, a division of Beyond The Fray, LLC, San Diego, CA

www.beyondthefraypublishing.com

34. Dulce Base	169
35. Danny Casolaro	175
36. Miriam Bush	179
37. Paul Parada	183
38. Tall Whites	191
39. The Bridge	195
40. The River Weaver Sighting	199
Afterword Gemma Jade	205
About the Author	209
Also by Gemma Jade	211

CONTENTS

Introduction   v
Gemma Jade

1. Messengers of Deception   1
2. The Carrot   7
3. The Talavera La Real Air Base Encounter   11
4. Alien Pancakes   15
5. Gustavo Gonzalez and Jose Ponce   19
6. The Magic Show   23
7. Pier Zanfretta   29
8. The Hopkinsville Incident   33
9. The La Rubia Incident   39
10. Whitley Streiber   43
11. Hilary Porter   47
12. Cherry Hinkle   51
13. The Grouse Mountain Incident   55
14. The Cunningham / Lovette Incident   63
15. Cisco Grove   67
16. Tossey / Begay   71
17. Lydia Morel   75
18. Filiberto Cardenas   77
19. Betty Luca   81
20. The Neighbors   85
21. The Ides of March Sightings / The Phoenix Lights   91
22. The Trial of Joe Moody   95
23. Joel Lankford   99
24. Children of the Grays   101
25. Minnie   109
26. Betty and Barney Hill (Part One)   113
27. Betty and Barney Hill (Part Two)   119
28. The Derbyshire BBQ   125
29. Helen Thomas and Her Mother Carol   127
30. Travis Walton (Part One)   131
31. Travis Walton (Part Two)   141
32. Travis Walton (Part Three)   151
33. Acapulco Abduction   161

INTRODUCTION

GEMMA JADE

While it's true I've built a career about discussing my own experiences with beings from other realms and dimensions, and then expanded on that to recounting other people's strange encounters with creatures of all types, some known but most unknown, the truth is up until very recently extraterrestrials didn't ever really catch my interest. However, an experience I had on Mother's Day of 2022 changed all of that and I've been on the hunt ever since for people who have had encounters similar to mine. I'll go through that encounter at some point in this book and while I haven't really found anyone who has had any similar experiences to the one I had, I have found so many people who have had encounters with creatures and beings that could not possibly be from our planet. Most of the stories include so-called "known" aliens but some of the stories you are about to read will seem unbelievable, but that's one of the main reasons I wanted to get these out there. Not enough people are willing to talk about their experiences and I feel like, now in 2025, we have nothing to lose and everything to gain from being open and honest about what we've been through, our thoughts and feelings about extraterrestrials as a whole, and possibly even what's really going on beyond the barriers of our own planet and our own existence in the universe. Some of these encounters I've found in historical records and I urge all of you who read this to do your own research and form your own opinions. I do not claim to have the answers as to what we are dealing with in any individual experience or with alien entities as a whole, but I know that being silent never helps when we're seeking the truth. With that said I hope you enjoy this book and if you've had an encounter with any extraterrestrial creatures, provided you can remember it at all, I urge you as well to talk about it and let the world know your story. I decided a long time ago that keeping all of my encounters and experiences to myself was doing nothing for me and that's just another reason why I choose to write about the topics I do; because, if nothing else, I am more than willing to be the voice for people too fearful to come forward. I know all too well what that feels like. But, I hope this book will prove to you that you are not alone, and that WE aren't alone in the universe, in this realm, or beyond....

CHAPTER 1
MESSENGERS OF DECEPTION

Jaume Jacques Bordas' amazing story was first publicized by a Spanish researcher named Antonio Ribera and that was in 1971. However, it wasn't until it was then picked up by another researcher named Jacques Vallee who included it in his published works, a book called "Messengers of Deception" that the story really started to get around. Jaume Jacques Bordas was born on July 20th, 1911, an astrological Cancer, and for most of his childhood he was very sickly and weak. He was said to have some sort of hormonal deficiency or imbalance, which experts today believe could have been something with his thyroid, and it caused him to suffer severe weight gain and then he wouldn't be able to lose any weight, no matter how hard his parents tried or what his diet was. His pituitary condition made it so that he was also developmentally slow which caused him some issues at school, mainly with him having an impaired attention span and being unable to pay attention at all or for very long.

One night when he was twelve years old, Jacques felt like he was being compelled to climb to the terrace of his home. He hadn't ever done that before and there was no reason that night would be different from any other but he couldn't help himself. It was inexplicable and he insisted he felt as though he'd had no control over his decision, but he obeyed and climbed up there anyway. When he got up on the terrace, something spectacular and amazing happened. He saw a group of small, triangular objects that to him looked like tiny little planes flying around, all across the sky above him. Three of those crafts, which measured a total of less than nine feet in length, dropped down and landed near him. One of them opened up like a fan and out walked a being about his size, maybe a bit smaller, wearing a white suit and a bright white cloak. It spoke to Jacques, saying, "We have come to see you, because we have taken you under our protection. We know how much you suffer, and we know your dream of becoming a strong man, an athlete. You will realize it, with our help; you will be strong, not only physically but mentally, too. Now that we have adopted you, we will never forsake you. In the future we will come back to you again. In the meantime, as a token of friendship, take this."

So, before we go any further I will say I am no expert on extraterrestrials and how they work and don't know very much about why they operate the way they do most of the time. However, in all the extensive research I've done just in the last few years, I wonder if Jacques wasn't a part of their kin, in their bloodline- somewhere down the line in history. This frustrates me a bit because we will never know the why's of it all and I would love to know that more than anything else. Meaning, I feel like I need to know how and why they chose him. However, as of writing this, I've found no additional information. The being who had spoken to him then handed Jacques what looked like a small, square piece of dark candy and told the young boy to make sure he ate the candy- all of it at once- because it was going to mark the beginning of a whole new life and a whole new world would open up for him as a result as well. So, obviously Jacques never read my book "Missing: The Fae Theory" where I reiterate over and over again that one must never accept gifts or food from a fairy and even though ETs aren't fairies, I feel like that warning should fit here too. However, he ate the whole thing right then and there as he had been instructed to do.

The being got back into the "airplane" and all of them shot back off into the night sky again, disappearing. Jacques simply turned and went back to his bedroom after that and went to sleep and the encounter picked up with him waking up the next morning with the taste of something like tar in his mouth. For him, this proved that the whole amazing encounter from the night before hadn't only been a dream. Not that he needed it, but more proof would come over the course of the next four years too, as he went through a seemingly impossible and absolutely remarkable physical transformation. He grew incredibly strong and all the extra weight basically fell off of him. His mind had been equally fortified and he developed an interest in science and also, in mountains. Eventually he would go on to become an expert mountain climber and he accomplished many feats in that area. In 1934 Jacques became the first Spaniard to climb to the top of the Aiguille Verte in the French Alps. In 1937 he crossed the Grand Jura and ascended Grand Chervoz. Just as he had been told he would, Jacques had many other interactions with non-human entities throughout his lifetime. He lived to be one hundred years old! I couldn't possibly go through the hundreds of encounters here in this short chapter but I will give you some of the ones that stuck out to me and that are most often talked about when his extraordinary story is discussed.

In 1951 Jacques was resting out on his patio when he was approached by a man who was about six feet tall, had long blonde hair, bright blue eyes and who was extremely pale. The "man's" eyes were described as being "slightly elongated." The man asked Jacques if he would be willing to provide him with two bottles of milk and some bread. Jacques agreed and the men met every day at the same time and place and he brought the food and drink with him each time. Finally, after a long time of this arrangement going on, Jacques asked the man where he was from to which he replied, "from above." Bordas thought the man meant he was from the mountain, and that the stranger was doing some sort of survey of the mountain and surrounding area. However, the strange man eventually showed Jacques a piece of parchment- like paper that had the mountains drawn on it in very fine detail. It also had on it a bunch of strange symbols and markings. Later on, when the subject of their conversation turned political, the stranger said, "Man must tear away his egotism. Man believes that he is unable to do this, but he can, although it's very hard. Man believes he is the only important being on the Earth; he ignores the fact that he is nothing more than one element in natural evolution. In spite of his unbounded pride, his so-called knowledge, there is another species evolving now that will replace him in due time. Even your children are undergoing the transformation: they will change everything, the religion."

On the last day he visited, the stranger repaid Jacques for his kindness and told him that while he had no actual money, he thought "his people," meaning human beings, would appreciate the gift. He gave him some solid chunks of gold he had found in the mountains during his travels. The stranger disappeared. Right after that all happened with the stranger, Jacques became very psychic in that he was particularly able to locate psychically any objects he or anyone else had lost or misplaced. He developed other psychic abilities as well. Twenty years later, in 1971, he received a phone call from that same stranger in which he explained that Jacques was about to experience further transformation. Jacques was told that his consciousness would now be open to "universal truths." There are many contacts between Jacques and this mysterious stranger but like I said I am trying to save time here. By the way I got this extra information from the book I mentioned earlier that was written by Jacques Vallee.

At the time the author met Jacques Bordas, he was a highly successful businessman, working at a furniture company in Andorra, exporting to more than thirty other countries. Upon further investigation into his story, Vallee was able to verify through many witnesses that Bordas was seen from time to time with a mysterious stranger who looked exactly like the man he had described who had given him the gold. The jeweler also verified that Jacques had brought some gold in for him to appraise. It was real gold and had been worth a lot of money. When Jacques Bordas' son took photos of family gatherings and picnics, all of the photos came out crystal clear except for the ones where the handsome and mysterious stranger had been in them. Most of those photos came out completely blank. Vallee interviewed Bordas in 1976 and found him to be very quiet and low key. He was a successful businessman who never even thought to try and make money off of his otherworldly contact. I'm not so sure Bordas had really known who or what he was dealing with but I'm sure not every single bit and piece of information about the exchanges between him and the stranger are publicized. There ended up being more than one of this odd looking man. In fact, there were several of them and he was friends with them all. Finally he asked where they were from and they responded that they were from the moon Titan, which orbits the planet Saturn.

I believe that Jacques was a part of these being's family somehow and might have chosen to be incarnated here for a reason, some reason to help their bloodline or race, something like that, but in having the extraterrestrial DNA plus that of his human parent or parents, maybe that's why he was born so ill in the first place. Maybe they felt an obligation to him to help him out, to watch over and befriend him. Of course this is all speculation on my part and I more than likely couldn't even begin to imagine what was actually taking place here or why.

CHAPTER 2
THE CARROT

This is definitely one of the most bizarre and outlandish cases of people who claimed to have had an encounter with extraterrestrial beings I have ever come across. I found it in a book by Timothy Beckley called Strange Effects of Flying Saucers and it's said to have happened in the summer of 1967. The moon was shining large and brightly in the sky in some desert that's still unnamed to this day, out in California and it happened in the early hours of the morning. It was dark outside when eighteen year old Jerry James, along with his parents and younger sister were driving through what locals call "the badlands." They were headed from their home in Colorado to a vacation home they kept in California. The whole family was excited to be going to Cali and the mood in the car was upbeat and reflected that excitement. They were having fun and getting along well, despite the fact that they had been in the car for almost eighteen hours at that point. They drove a Chevy pick-up and were pulling a house trailer. They needed to stop and so they pulled into a rest area and got out to stretch their legs. It was the last leg of their journey and none of them could wait to get where they were going already.

It only took seconds for the whole family to notice the strange object hovering in the distance in the night sky above them. At first they just assumed it was some sort of normal aircraft but they quickly realized that wasn't the case. It was somewhat spherical, the size of an average vehicle and it resembled one of those top toys as it was spinning around in the sky as though it were on some sort of axis or something. It was just wandering around at first and the family watched but they started to absolutely panic when the craft emitted a very bright beam of light, like a giant flashlight in the sky, and as the beam suddenly and continuously began wandering all around the desert below it and all around them. It was as if it were searching for something down there. The family could only stare at it, totally bewildered and a bit fright-ened, for a few minutes but once the beam trained and shined down right onto them, their fright turned to all out terror as they wondered what in the world was going on. The UFO sped through the sky in order to spin and hover directly above them and the light was so bright the family recalled that it was as though suddenly it was broad daylight out there instead of the wee hours of the morning. The family and the craft were completely silent during the whole ordeal, as they waited in fear to see what would happen next. Just as the family started to enter-tain the idea that they were possibly in for some big time trouble, the beam of blinding light suddenly went dark as though someone had merely flipped a light switch and the craft took off at incredible speeds into the night sky. The family were confused and really scared, rightfully so, but they had no idea that the worst, and the weirdest part of their ordeal, was yet to come.

The next day the family was once again a few miles from that same service station and they got out once again to stretch their legs. I was wondering about this so I looked it up and it turned out they hadn't continued through to California yet and stopped somewhere for the night, making it so that they had to pass that service station again before moving on to their vacation home. They almost immediately noticed a vessel that looked like it was silver in color as it came speeding through the sky right towards them. It was so close that they all said they could not only see it much more clearly than the night before, but could have probably counted all the little rivets on the sides and all around the craft as well. The craft was metallic and as it hovered above the family, the mother was so terrified she crumpled to the ground in a heap. She fainted right there on the spot. She had to be revived with smelling salts and as soon as she was up and moving again, the family decided that it would be a good idea to go into their trailer to hide and wait out whatever was happening. However, once they went to the back of the vehicle where the trailer was, they saw that a surprise was waiting for them there too. Just moments earlier, when they had initially exited it, the place had been a mess. Their beds were unmade and there were dirty dishes and clothes all over the place. They had just woken up and no one had cleaned anything up yet. The entire trailer was not only spotless but pristine with all the dishes done, the beds neatly and expertly made and the whole trailer sparkling clean. Everything was put away, almost like, while they were all standing right there and stretching their legs out for those few moments, someone had gone inside and worked some sort of magic. Even if it had been a person who had gotten in, surely the family definitely would have noticed. There was only one thing that was out of place and that was a lone dish on their counter that had something inside of it.

The family walked over to the dish and stared confusedly at what looked like a sprouting carrot. However, the "carrot" started to transform and move around right before their very eyes and they all saw it doing so. It sprouted roots but the way that they moved reminded the family more of tentacles than anything else and those tentacle roots grew quickly as the "carrot" or whatever it was, fell to the ground and started writing around. It was ever expanding and becoming tangled as it grew, causing the terrified family to keep stepping back in order to avoid becoming entangled in it all. The plant, the dish it had originally sat upon and the cabinet near it were all covered in some sort of slimy, green goop substance. Jerry said about it, "It was a vile smelling substance, and other than that I can't tell you much about it. One thing was strange though. When I touched it with a pencil it 'ate up' the wood and lead in a matter of seconds."

I don't know the exact timing of all of this but the family did eventually get back on the road. They couldn't just stay there at that rest stop all day, right? However, as he drove, the father noticed that he wasn't in control of the vehicle anymore and it would not only accelerate of its own accord but it would also brake and move all around on its own as well. They reached another service station eventually and pulled in to get some gas. When they pulled the gas cap off it made a noise as though it were burping and a nasty smell came hissing out of it. Making things even stranger was the fact that the driver's seat seemed to have melted or eroded away somehow and was barely there anymore. The ignition key glowed in the dark and had somehow become rubber-like in its malleability. This case is completely and totally baffling but more than that, there's no more information at all so I assume they weren't abducted or at least, to the best of their collective and individual knowledge they weren't, because I looked and looked and couldn't find anything at all about this case other than what I just told you. My guess is that it was just an odd and freakish occurrence and the family were eventually able to move on with their lives. Who can really know for sure though and it makes me wonder if it's true, then why is there nothing else online or anywhere else about it? Could it be being suppressed? My money is on yes, it definitely is.

CHAPTER 3
THE TALAVERA LA REAL AIR BASE ENCOUNTER

In scouring the internet for real encounters with extraterrestrials and their crafts, I found a fairly terrifying one in the country of Spain. It's a rather violent encounter that allegedly happened in the city of Badajoz. This city has been occupied since the Bronze Age and has been the subject of many wars between Spain and Portugal. It's a very popular tourist destination for that region and not somewhere you would immediately think of when you think of encounters with aliens. With that being said, in 1976 it became the place where one of the most bizarre encounters with extraterrestrials on record has ever happened, before or since, in the entire country. On November 12, 1976 at around one forty five in the morning two two soldiers who worked at the Talavera La Real Air Base, and whose names were Jose Maria Trejo and Juan Carrizosa Lujan were on patrol at the area of the base where the fuel was stored and up to that point they'd been having a fairly normal and somewhat boring night. Typically while these two men were on duty nothing ever happened and they themselves had said that the nights were always uneventful. However, on this night, everything would change.

The two men were just walking around, patrolling the area, as was their duty when they were both snapped out of whatever thoughts they had been having by a blaring noise of what sounded to them like some sort of static or radio interference. The two men immediately thought that they were dealing with trespassers and wasted no time in looking for whoever it was but as they searched the sound got much louder and much more intense. It quickly transformed from a droning static to a high pitched whistling noise and throughout the next few minutes it became more high pitched and so much louder. After about five minutes of building in volume and intensity it suddenly stopped and there was an eerie silence that the two men were left to contemplate when it was all over. The men still weren't sure what in the world was happening and continued to patrol with their weapons at the ready. They knew that something very strange was happening and as they moved through the base, the sound returned suddenly and all at once to such a degree that the men were all but incapacitated by it. Whatever it was finally stopped again and as soon as it did the men saw a light shining down from the sky vertically but they described it too as being like a flash of light that lasted for about thirty seconds and then vanished as well.

As all of this was happening another guard arrived, this one had a dog with him, and he said that he had also seen and heard some pretty strange things. The men radioed the information of the events in to their superiors and were ordered to do a sweep of the entire base. They searched methodically, walking parallel to a large wall that separated the main road from the base. Everything was quiet and the dog was calm for a few minutes but after walking several hundred yards the sound of snapping twigs and sticks, along with a vortex of air passing near them, caused them to let the dog go so that it could investigate the area where the noises and the air had come from on its own while they stood back a little bit and watched. The dog ran off into the darkness but quickly returned, seemingly dizzy, disoriented and nauseous. Despite it being sick, the dog once again ran towards the same area and again came back stumbling around and unable to walk properly. It only took a moment for the dog to return to its normal self and when it did it circled the men in a maneuver it had been trained to do when it was alerting its handlers to an outside threat and letting them know it needed to protect them.

With that, the men held their weapons aimed at the darkness as they huddled close to one another and stared into the blackness expectantly, waiting for someone or something to emerge that their dog had already deemed threatening. The dog continued circling around them as a human shaped, glowing green light appeared in the darkness where the activity seemed to be. The figure slowly walked closer to the men and it didn't take long for them to realize that they were looking at some sort of other-worldly entity that stood at ten feet tall or more and seemed to be composed of millions of small light points. The brightness of it was more intense around the edges. The entity was described as wearing a helmet on its glowing green head and having freakishly long arms and legs but no hands or feet. Mister Trejo fainted but before he could even hit the ground one of the other men had opened fire on the entity. The entity seemed impervious to the fifty or more rounds the soldier pumped into it except that it glowed brighter each time one of the bullets struck it before it seemingly flashed incredibly brightly for a second and then vanished into thin air right before their eyes. Immediately after the entity had vanished into thin air, that same whistling noise pierced the air for about fifteen seconds before it was eerily still and quiet out there again and then the men set about helping their fallen friend. They got Trejo back to the base and that was that for the rest of the night.

The following morning more than fifty soldiers searched the entire property of the base to try and locate the strange entity but not only didn't they find any sign of it, they found no bullets, no casings and upon further and closer inspection of the man who did the firing's weapon, it hadn't even been discharged at all. The base was obviously put on high alert for several days following the intrusion but nothing happened and eventually Trejo would regain consciousness again. However, a few days later he lost his vision and slumped to the floor in the mess hall. He was treated and had no further episodes but the doctors could never figure out what had been the cause of his strange illnesses or the temporary blindness in the first place. The incident would go on to be chalked up to a joint hallucination between the three men and, apparently the dog, brought on by stress, lack of sleep and panic and not too long after it was seemingly all but forgotten about. I know most of you were thinking something different, but when I said it was a violent encounter, I meant by the soldiers in that they shot this unknown being with more than fifty rounds when it hadn't done anything except make the dog a little bit sick for just a few seconds. This is why other entities, bigfoot and most aliens included, do not want human beings having any sort of proof of their existence. At least, that's my take on it anyway.

CHAPTER 4
ALIEN PANCAKES

It all started on the morning of April 18, 1961 in a rural area of Wisconsin called Eagle River. On that morning a sixty year old chicken farmer by the name of Joe Simonton sat down on his porch to have himself some breakfast. The morning was calm and tranquil but was about to take a turn for the highly strange if I ever did see one. He sat there, slowly eating, drinking his coffee and looking out over his chickens, when the peaceful morning was shattered by a loud sound that Joe himself described as being like "knobby tires on wet pavement." The noise seemed to have been coming from behind the house and it was strange enough to him that he immediately got up and went to investigate it. When he did so he saw a silver disc that was about twelve feet high and about thirty feet in diameter. It had something similar to exhaust pipes coming out of the side and Joe watched as it came down out of the sky and began to hover directly over his property. A hatch opened on the bottom of the craft and three little men with dark skin, that stood at around five feet tall and were all dressed identically in what looked like two piece black suits, turtlenecks and helmets stepped out of it. Joe said the strange little men were "Italian looking" and were holding something that looked to him like a jug. The beings didn't hesitate in approaching him and gestured towards the little jug and even though they didn't actually speak or say anything, Joe was telepathically told that he needed to fill the jug with water for them. He took it from them and said about it that it was, "a beautiful thing. A Thermos jug-like bottle unlike any jug I have ever seen here on Earth." As he began filling the jig with water the beings pulled something out of the craft that Joe described as looking like a flameless gas grill and when he returned with the full jug the beings looked hard at work preparing something on that grill-like object. Upon closer inspection Joe said that it was food food and looked something like what we call pancakes. The beings then stacked the "pancakes" on top of one another. Each one was about three inches in diameter and had little holes throughout them and they presented the stack to Joe before saluting him and getting back in their craft. The craft then took off into the sunny morning sky at such a speed that it was "gone in two seconds" according to the befuddled chicken farmer.

He later told reporters, "If that was their food, God help them, because I took a bite of one of them and it tasted like a piece of cardboard. If that's what they lived on, no wonder they were small. ... When they left I stood there in the driveway with a pile of greasy pancakes and my mouth open wondering what the heck I just saw, what happened." Even though Joe's story sounded too crazy to be true, other people in the area reported having seen that same exact craft and once they came forward it seemed like all of the United States had its eyes on this sleepy little town in the middle of nowhere in Wisconsin. The United States Air Force were the ones who were really focusing on the event, for whatever reason, and the National Investigating Committee for Aerial Phenomena were assisting them. The "pancakes" were analyzed by the Food and Drug Laboratory of the United States Department of Health, Education and Welfare who came to the rather disappointing and mundane conclusion that they had been made up of hydrogenated fat, cornstarch, buckwheat hulls, soya bean hulls and wheat bran. I know that's not what anyone was expecting but does that mean that they weren't made by aliens? Not in my opinion.

Most people will say that even if this case doesn't disprove aliens exist it doesn't prove that they do either and as all of this was happening newspapers from all over the country were mockingly reporting on the incident and making a laughing stock out of poor Joe Simonton. He stuck to his story though and didn't care who believed him. In fact, a US Air Force Investigator, named J. Allen Hynek came to the conclusion that at the very least, Joe believed what he was saying. Hynek said, "There is no question that Mr. Simonton felt that his contact had been a real experience. Simonton answered questions directly, did not contradict himself, insisted on the facts being exactly as he stated and refused to accept embellishments or modifications. He stated he was sure that we wouldn't believe him but that he didn't care whether he was believed. He stated simply that this happened and that was that. He appeared quite sincere to me, and did not appear to be the perpetrator of a hoax."

I found some information that was hidden in the bowels of only a handful of case studies that were done on this encounter that weren't included in the large majority of them and that's that in the months that followed his encounter, Joe's chickens got sick and almost all of them died. He was absolutely sure that the encounter with the strange beings had everything to do with the death of his chickens and he would tell a friend of his, Judge Frank W. Carter, all about it. Carter would then write, "Simonton informed me that twenty three chickens had died since April 18th and thought maybe that may have been caused by the alleged Saucer. He sells eggs to customers in town here, and the sheriff, County Agricultural Agent and myself drove out, from a Health standpoint, to see IF the eggs might be affected by radiation. We took one diseased chicken to a local vet who "thought" the chicken MIGHT be sick from food deficiency, and that they'd been becoming cannibals, pecking at each other, where feathers drop off and kill each other. No Geiger was used however." As far as the Air Force was concerned the case was just simply forgotten about and not really ever mentioned again after they decided it was simply "unexplained."

CHAPTER 5
GUSTAVO GONZALEZ
AND JOSE PONCE

In 1954 in Petare, Venezuela there were two men who were driving in a van to a pork wholesaler store, late at night and for whatever reason. The men were almost abducted by aliens that night and who knows what would have happened to them had they not fought back. I haven't been able to find any more info about the aliens who allegedly went after them that night either so who knows what they were up to. It was later reported that the road suddenly became completely blocked by a "glowing sphere." There was absolutely no way for the two men, named Gustavo Gonzalez and Jose Ponce, to get around the UFO, even if they had had the time to do so, which they did not. Immediately upon coming to a complete stop and I'm sure wondering what the hell was going on, three short and very hairy aliens came out of the craft and started towards them. For some reason this amazing and incredibly interesting case isn't very well documented and has kind of gotten lost to history and/or lack of retelling but here is what I know. The three aliens, who I keep imagining by the way they were described as looking like Wookies from the Star Wars movies, made some kind of abduction attempt on the two friends. However, they got the wrong two men that night and both Ponce and Gonzalez fought back with all of their might and soul.

Gonzalez even pulled out a pocket knife, allegedly his knife from his old days in the Boy Scouts of all things, and tried, in vain, to stab at least one of these beings. The stabs didn't penetrate the aliens skin, however, as underneath the hair it appeared they had extremely rough or as it was later described, "rhinoceros like" skin. After some punching and kicking, knocking the aliens off one another's backs, etc, the men were able to run back to their vehicle and get away, relatively unscathed. I keep just thinking of it like a bar room brawl but with some super short hairy guys and two grown and regular sized men, one of which had a knife. Now, you may ask, due to my growing sarcasm while recounting this encounter, why I chose to put it in the book here. Well, I actually believe it and I wanted to include it here because for me it shows how some encounters have almost no information out there about them but that doesn't mean they didn't happen and it makes me very nervous about the fact that these types of violent abductions or abduction attempts are taking place in the first place.

I know some of y'all are gonna point out that they don't have the Boy Scouts in Venezuela, but I am just reporting the facts as I have read and believe them. Perhaps Gonzalez was in something similar to our Boy Scouts here in America OR perhaps, and even more likely, that bit got added in by some smart ass who thought this was all some kind of joke or hoax. Either way though he really did pull out a pocket knife. Why did the aliens retreat? Couldn't they just put these two to sleep telepathically or however they do it? Couldn't they have put out that overwhelming sense of peace and safety most other aliens are known to be able to do very well and also, very often? I don't know, honestly, and I am still searching for what kind of alien race this could possibly have been. I have gotten a lot of comments in the video I did about this case on my youtube channel about the correlation between Bigfoot and extraterrestrials but I hace to say, Bigfoot isn't the only sometimes tall, sometimes very short, hairy beasts roaming among us that we don't know if it actually exists. This encounter story demonstrates that. I don't think it was a group of Bigfoot coming off an alien craft that night, but can I say for certain? No. Many people have accused these two men of making the whole thing up just to get attention and possibly money but that's what "they" always say, right? I'm just not ready to discount this encounter so easily.

CHAPTER 6
THE MAGIC SHOW

At first I wasn't sure if I wanted to add my own personal encounters to the compilation in this book and whether I add anymore or not time will tell but I was thinking about it last night and while doing some research online I found a couple of people who have had similar encounters to the one I had just this past June, in 2025, and knowing that makes me feel much more comfortable sharing than I normally would. I grew up surrounded by the paranormal and am completely in my element when it comes to talking about spirits and entities from other worlds and realms, but when it comes to extraterrestrials, I am a bit out of my element because I feel like it's all so massive and hard for me to understand. Anyway, here is one of my encounters.

Every year in my town, in the Spring and Summer seasons we have all sorts of county and town fairs and I try to go to as many of them as possible because I love the whole atmosphere of them. They remind me of a simpler time, even with the insane prices nowadays, and the simpler time I'm speaking of is one I've only seen in movies or read about in books. This past June there was a little carnival being held within walking distance of my home and I decided to go on opening night. I knew it would be busy but I was excited about it and didn't want to wait until the next day to go. I actually would end up going all four days, but that's a different story altogether. I got some carnival food and went on a ride or two and then I heard the announcement that there would be a magician on the stage in the back of the place a little later on in the night. The magician would be going on to perform right around dusk and I decided that I would stay and watch the show. I wandered around a little more and by the time I got to the back of the facility, away from most of the rest of the carnival and to where the show was going to be starting any minute, the whole area was filled with people. This made sense because the whole reason I almost never go to the fairs or carnivals on opening night in the first place is because of how crowded it will inevitably be. It was a warm Thursday night and while there was a nice breeze, there wasn't a chill in the air at all, which will be important a little later on.

I filed into the group of about a hundred or so people waiting to see the magic act and within minutes of it starting the sun started to go down. I was just looking around me because I always try to be aware of my surroundings and everything looked normal, at first. Then, suddenly, a cold chill went through my body and I started to feel fearful for seemingly no reason. My breathing got heavy and labored, goosebumps prickled on my arms and the hair on the back of my neck stood up. There were no spiritual presences around aside from the "usual" deceased person who had wandered in and was walking around, but I see them all of the time and almost everywhere I go. If you haven't seen my YouTube channel or read any of my other books, you would know that this is nothing new for me to see and experience and it defi-nitely was not the reason I was suddenly feeling the way that I was. It was like the crowd was closing in on me and I had to close my eyes and take some deep breaths to stop everything from spinning. I could faintly hear people clapping for the magician and his assistant on the stage as they performed a few tricks that the people around me seemed to be getting a kick out of. I started to feel a little better. I took a few sips of my fresh squeezed lemonade and looked around again. The moment seemed to have passed and I was relieved. I looked at the stage and the magician was pulling something out of his hat, to the amazement of the crowd and his assistant. I remember that it wasn't a rabbit, but I don't remember exactly what it was. Then he asked for a volunteer. Normally I would volunteer but there were tons of kids around so I smiled at how eager they all were and I was still looking around and smiling when I saw something that seemed odd to me, though I couldn't put my finger on why.

As a little boy happily made his way up onto the stage, I saw someone two rows in front of me and to my left, who was incredibly tall. It caught my eye because I am five foot seven and this man had to have been at least seven feet tall or more. It wasn't scary in and of itself, or at least it shouldn't have been, but I found myself lingering on this person and unable to take my eyes off the back of his head. He had long, colorful dreadlocks pulled up high on his head into a ponytail and he was wearing a bright red shirt. I suddenly couldn't breathe again and I felt as though the wind had been knocked out of me. I finally looked away and immediately felt better again, as the little kid was trying to pull apart two giant rings that looked easier to pull apart than they were. They were in the middle of a trick. I looked back at the man and this time he was looking at me. He wasn't just looking at me either, he was staring at me, and he was smirking. It wasn't a pleasant smile or even a cute smirk, it penetrated my spirit. It was absolutely evil. I tried to look away but couldn't.

The tall white man turned away from me as the crowd was oohing and ahhing at the show and clapping for the little kid, who was still trying to pull those rings apart. The magician kept pulling them apart and reattaching them, and then challenging the kid to pull them apart. He had done it so easily, and again, that must have been the trick. I inevitably looked back over to the man and that's when something terrifying happened. The entire event went silent and still and no one and nothing was moving at all. Time stopped and stood still, all except for me, it seemed. However, that wasn't the case and I instinctively knew it. I looked back again over to the tall man with the dreadlocks and he was no longer a man. He was a seven foot tall, green and scaly reptilian creature, looking at me with those sinister and creepy eyes and flicking his lizard tongue out at me. I couldn't even scream. I was so terrified. My knees started to shake and buckle under me and he looked like he was smiling. I tried to back away but while his gaze was on me I couldn't move at all. I was seemingly just as stuck as everyone else in the whole fair around me. The rides had stopped completely in mid air, people's drinks were held to their lips. Some were caught mid-clap and mid-laugh, and there was nothing I could do but hold this thing's gaze and shudder in fear. Finally, he turned back towards the stage and everything immediately went back to normal. Normal… but not.

The magician and the boy were now doing something with cards, the reptilian creature disguised as a man had his disguise back on and looked like nothing more than a very tall man in a crowd, and I was incredibly confused. The sun had fully set and although everyone and everything had stopped moving, although time had stood still, it hadn't. The trick with the rings was over and they'd moved on to some sort of card trick and no one seemed to have noticed what happened except for me. I turned and made my way as quickly as I could out of that crowd and out of the carnival completely. I had to walk home, in the dark, and the entire way I had to walk on a road with no streetlights and no sidewalks. I was terrified the entire time but I made it home without incident. Just as I was putting the key into my front door though I started to lose my breath again and I felt like I was going to pass out. I knew, without even turning around or looking back, that creature was somewhere around me and had probably followed me home. I don't know to what end because I didn't see it again at that time and haven't since. I went back to the fair the next three nights in a row, even though I was scared to run into it again, but I didn't and it didn't seem to be there at all on those days. However, I believe these things walk around us at all times and at any given time we could be near one and not really notice. I do believe they have some sort of effects on our spirit which manifests into physical symptoms, like my labored breathing and being unable to keep my knees from buckling, but if we aren't looking directly at them then we probably won't even notice. Even if we do look right at them, the overwhelming sensations that take over our bodies when we do is probably just the distraction they need for us to look away and for them to slink back to wherever it is they came from, or at least to get them away from us and stop us from noticing what they are. This wasn't the first time I've had an experience with these particular creatures and I have a terrible feeling it won't be the last either. So, I guess I could honestly say that this one is more than likely to be continued.

CHAPTER 7
PIER ZANFRETTA

On the night of December 6th, 1978 in the village of Torriglia in Italy, a night watchman named Pier Zanfretta was on one of his routine patrols when he encountered something not only out of this world but really, REALLY bizarre. Pier didn't have just one encounter though, he had a series of them and by the end of it he was questioning his own sanity. Our witness was on his way to a client's home. The client wasn't there but Pier was doing his due diligence and making sure the home was protected from intruders and really anything else that would come along and disturb the property while the homeowners were gone. On his way to this client's house his car suddenly and inexplicably lost power and Pier had to pull over onto the side of the road, within eyesight of the client's house, and see what was going on with his vehicle. Before he got out of his car though he looked through the window and saw something strange and out of place. He said he looked through the driver's side window of his car and saw four small lights moving around the backyard of the house he was supposed to be inspecting.

Our witness immediately assumed that these beams were coming from flashlights and so he got out of his car with his revolver and flashlight in hand. He, of course, assumed that these people who were holding what he thought were flashlights were trespassers and so he decided to very stealthily approach the property. After all he thought there were four of them and, despite his weapon, he was only one man. Perhaps he imagined that these were intruders and that's exactly what his job was- it was to protect the property from this exact thing. Right when he was about to jump out and surprise the trespassers though, he felt something tap him on the back. He immediately turned around and was confronted with some being that he described as, "An enormous green, ugly and frightful creature, with undulating skin... as though he were very fat or dressed in a loose, gray tunic... no less than 10-feet tall."

There were two others as well. Two of the exact same creatures were standing, one on each side of the being that had tapped his shoulder. Our witness further described the creatures as being hairy, having horns on the sides of their faces, green skin, triangular shaped eyes that glowed a bright yellow and red veins that looked to be always there on their foreheads. The mouths of the creatures were most shocking of all because they all had this weird equipment that was self illuminating and fit over the mouth- reminiscent of oxygen/breathing apparatuses that we use here on Earth. Pier was shocked and terrified and tried his best to quickly get back to his car and away from the entities. However, as he approached his car a light came from behind him and when he looked over his shoulder to see where it was coming from, he saw a massive UFO slowly descending from the night sky above. He explained he heard a loud hissing noise that came from the craft and before he knew what was happening he was blasted with a huge gust or ray of extreme heat. He stumbled back to his car; shocked and in excruciating pain.

He contacted the security company that he worked for and the person who answered his pleas on the other end of the radio later recounted that Pier was babbling nonsensically and stuttering incoherently, saying things like, "they aren't men, they aren't men" and "By God they are UGLY!" About an hour later when the two other guards arrived, the ones who were called in for backup, they found Pier laying on the frozen ground and when they went to help him up they noticed that his clothes were still warm to the touch. Behind the house, in the backyard there were several horseshoe shaped markings that came from an extremely heavy object having been standing there. A little later, once this report came out, it was discovered that at least fifty two other residents of this small village saw a bright light coming from the exact same area where our witness had his otherworldly encounter. In the following months Pier claimed that he had consistently come across these same creatures. He also said there were other beings as well who he saw, along with the ones he described in the original account. He said he came across gigantic, non-human footprints where he lived and plenty of other tangible evidence he believes lends credibility to and backs up his original and subsequent claims. At least they do in my opinion.

CHAPTER 8
THE HOPKINSVILLE INCIDENT

On August 21, 1955 at approximately seven pm near Hopkinsville, Kentucky in the United States, a family named the Taylors were visiting with their friends, the Suttons when our next strange and bizarre encounter happened. The Suttons had a well on their property; a rustic farmhouse, and one of the Taylors, Billy Ray, went out to go and get some water from it. What happened next would change both of these families' lives forever. While Billy Ray was out there at the well, he saw what he described as a rainbow colored, gleaming and disc shaped object land in a gorge, just off the property about a mile away. He was scared and so he ran back as fast as he could to tell everyone else what he had just seen. His family and the Sutton family both laughed at him and insisted that what he had seen was nothing more than a shooting star. How someone could ever mistake what Billy Ray saw with a shooting star is beyond me but it just goes to show what I always say is true and completely demonstrates my point; people will create whatever they want and tell themselves whatever they can in order to explain away things like this. To explain away the unimaginable.

His family assured him that his eyes and his mind were playing tricks on him. They wouldn't be able to try and convince themselves or Billy Ray of this for long because a few moments later the Sutton's dogs started barking very aggressively, into the darkness outside. Taylor and Elmer Sutton grabbed their guns and decided to go and investigate what the dogs were barking about. They ran outside thinking perhaps that there was someone in their yard who didn't belong there and, in a way, they were exactly right- but it wasn't what any of them had expected. There was a three foot tall luminous being with glowing eyes, a giant and very oversized head, pointed and floppy ears, thin legs, a narrow mouth and talons as fingernails. The creature was floating just a few inches above the ground and was wearing a silver, metallic jumpsuit type thing. It immediately charged at the two men as they stood there with their guns aimed at it and also, they were trying to process what it was that they were seeing. The men were shocked and terrified so they fired their weapons as the creature charged at them with its hands in the air, however when the shots were fired the being did several backflips and disappeared into the woods; it seemed as though it had not been hit by any of the gunfire.

Taylor and Elmer ran as fast as they could back into the house. Before they could tell the others what had transpired though, the same being was spotted peering through the window of the farmhouse by the two men. The two men fired more shots at the thing, blasting right through the already opened, screened window, but when they ran outside there was no corpse or injured creature- there was nothing there and it seemed to have escaped the gunfire altogether again. There was no blood or anything- nothing at all except the remnants of the broken and blasted down screen window. A being that was either the exact same one or one very similar jumped down onto the men off of the awning over the porch and immediately entangled its gnarly and taloned fingers into someone's hair. Somehow it's said that despite it being entangled in the one man's hair with no intentions of letting go or giving up, they fired again but this being too just missed being shot and took off running into the surrounding woods. By now the men had been off the porch and chasing this creature into the woods, still firing their rifles at it and missing it every single time.

As they kept running after it there was suddenly a whole crew of these beings chasing after them as they now ran back to the farmhouse to inform the others of what was going on and what they had encountered. The beings were already running all over the rooftop of the farmhouse and were also appearing simultaneously in all of the windows both upstairs and down. There were eleven people, men, women and children in the tiny little home and they were all more terrified than they had ever been before. Bullets were doing absolutely nothing to affect these things, it's like they were completely and totally bulletproof- though no one could quite see how it was that the rounds were missing their targets completely. Finally, after three hours of being tormented by these beings who refused to get off of the roof and stop peeking through the windows; they were banging, clanging and making all kinds of noise throughout the outside of the house, the families had enough and decided to make a fast break for the two vehicles that were parked there outside. One of the kids who were there later reported that the creatures "stuck to the side of the house in the way a spider would." They did make it to the cars though and they drove immediately to the local Sheriff's station.

The Sheriff at that time was a man named Russell Greenwell and he and his deputies were there that night when the petrified families came running into the office, ranting and raving about what they had just experienced with these strange, otherworldly beings. They were quickly able to determine that no one was drunk or insane and that they were very credible eyewitnesses and so the sheriff and his deputies went back to the farmhouse with the two families and investigated the allegations. Sheriff Greenwell would later go on to say, "These were not the sort of people who normally ran to the police... something frightened them, something beyond their comprehension." Initially the officers noticed nothing that would back up the claims that the creatures had been there and only the remnants of all the shots fired seemed to remain. However some neighbors did report hearing all of the gun fire and an independent witness in the form of a Highway Patrolman reported seeing strange, "meteor-like objects" flying around in the sky above him that same night, "with a sound like artillery fire coming directly from them." This had allegedly been witnessed and heard a little earlier in the night than when the families experienced their terror involving the entities. So basically the "artillery fire" heard by the independent witness could not have been all of the shots fired by the rifles at the creatures because this happened before the encounter at the farmhouse.

The sheriff and his deputies, after doing a thorough search of the farmhouse and the surrounding area- mainly the woods, assured both the Taylors and the Suttons that there was nothing more to fear and that, most likely in their opinions, the worst was over for them. They all returned to the farmhouse at approximately 2:15 in the morning. Unfortunately it wasn't long before the creatures returned and started climbing around on the walls of the outside of the house and also, once again, peering into all of the windows separately. Once again as well the men didn't know what to do and started shooting again. I mean, I'm not sure exactly what I would be doing at this point, being just a regular person, like these families, who knew nothing about extraterrestrials and how to keep them at bay and from attacking. I'm sure I would be terrified but at the same time I don't know if I would want to keep shooting up my home or my friend's home because these creatures were again, seemingly impervious to bullets and gunfire anyway. The beings kept up their harassment until just about the time the sun began to come up on the horizon and then they left, never to return again. Not long after this incident the Suttons left the farmhouse where the incident occurred and moved to a different location. This incident has come to be known as the Hopkinsville Goblins incident. I have a major problem with that because as bizarre as these creatures looked, they look nothing like what an actual goblin looks like and goblins are fae creatures, not extraterrestrials. It is what it is though and that's all I have on that particular incident. I cannot even begin to guess at what these specific creatures wanted or what they were doing there that night. It scares me to even think about it.

CHAPTER 9
THE LA RUBIA INCIDENT

Our next encounter is called the La Rubia Incident and happened in Brazil in 1977. A bus driver named Antonio La Rubia was driving at around 2:15 in the morning on the night of September 15th, 1977. As he drove along he suddenly came upon a gigantic, hat shaped, lead colored object that he estimated was approximately two hundred and fifty feet across and it was just sitting there in a field on the outskirts of where his house was. However, before he could go anywhere he was suddenly paralyzed by an extremely bright, brilliant blue beam of light. He saw three entities before him, all three of them he described as "robots." Our witness claims that they were about four feet tall with very long antennas on their heads which were spinning all around, non-stop. Their heads were shaped like footballs but vertical and a horizontal line of tinted blue mirrors were attached to the head. Their one leg each extended into a sort of "platform" at the bottom. He described them further as being covered in "scales" that were the color of aluminum but not shiny- more like matte or dull. Their arms were similar to the trunks of elephants and tapered off into one single finger-like thing and they allegedly wore belts with a bunch of syringes attached to it.

Our witness stood there, still paralyzed by the light and also, I'm sure, by fear. As he watched the three beings came towards him but they weren't walking- they were floating towards him and hovering just above the ground. One of the entities took one of the syringe-like things and pointed it at our terrified witness. This seemed to enable it to raise him up off of the ground and float him towards the giant spaceship or craft. He was brought straight and directly into the craft and as he was being forcibly brought in that direction, he saw dozens of the same exact robot beings following him in. He was now inside the craft and made to sit down as all of the creatures dispersed; surrounding him. He was almost immediately moved into another room and this is when he said he felt the craft start taking off. He was in some sort of circular chamber and estimated there to be about two dozen robots in there with him at that time. He screamed at them, asking "what do you want? Who are you?"

As soon as our witness spoke the creatures all collapsed to the floor of the circular room and started using their finger-like appendages to hold their rotating antenna still. He was immediately immobilized by the blue beam of light again but as he sat there he saw, now that they were still, that the antennas were shaped like spoons. After this, I'm assuming this is once the robots regained their balance and composure, La Rubia claims that one of the entities took a spinning object and used it to take a sample of his blood. The blood was then placed in front of some sort of machine that looked like what we would call a piano and once that happened he was shown a series of strange images, I think in his mind's eye but I'm not really sure. The images were said to be a huge factory where these robot beings were seemingly manufacturing UFOs. It was definitely a mass production of the exact ship La Rubia claims to have seen and that he was sitting in, right at that moment. Other images were being shown to him as well. There was an old train that quickly disappeared into an old tunnel. An image of himself in the nude with an angry dog barking as one of these robots melted into nothing right before his eyes. Apparently these objects would appear directly on the wall in front of our witness when one of the robots inserted one of the "syringes" into the "piano."

All of the sudden and without any warning our witness was suddenly crashing down into the road from high up in the air. It's like he was tossed or fell out of the spaceship. He soon realized he was in the city of Paciencia and he had all of his belongings with him and his watch had stopped as well. When he looked up he saw what he thought to be the bottom of the ship shooting very fast back into the sky. He described it as looking like, "a huge, dark balloon." The only other witness to this besides La Rubia was the town drunk and unfortunately he did not lend any more credibility to the encounter- at least as far as what he saw. He claimed to have seen our witness fall from a flying ship that then quickly ascended back towards the sky. Again though, that did nothing for most people as far as lending credibility to the initial encounter.

CHAPTER 10
WHITLEY STREIBER

Many of you might recognize the name in the title of this encounter story and I have to say this is one of the encounters that got me hooked into the extraterrestrial community and all of the various goings-on in it. On December 26, 1985 Whitley Streiber was just hanging out and having some rest and relaxation time to himself in a cabin in the woods when he was allegedly abducted by aliens. Streiber was an accomplished and well known writer and novelist and many of his writings were actually adapted into movies. According to friends you couldn't find a more logical person than Whitley. Lucky for us, he wrote all about the abduction in great detail, I'll go over the basics with you now.

Whitley was with his wife and son in this cabin and they were still somewhat celebrating the Christmas holiday and having some family time. For some unknown reason, Whitley had recently become paranoid of intruders and had installed a very high tech (at least for 1985) alarm system throughout his house and the cabin as well. At around 11pm, the day after Christmas, he activated the alarm system in his cabin and he and his family went to bed for the night. He claims that next he was awakened by some strange and unknown sound, he said he'd had "a gut feeling" that someone or something had breached his security measures.

Suddenly he was fully awake and absolutely horrified to see a strange creature standing there in his room at the foot of his bed, the bed he was sharing with his wife. He blinked and the next thing he could remember was sitting outside in the woods near his cabin. With his memories being sparse and fragmented he was absolutely terrified and didn't know quite what to do, and more importantly, he didn't know what in the world had just happened. It seemed, at that moment at least, that it was just the blink of an eye and he was there, in the woods outside.

He decided that he couldn't live with not knowing what had happened to him that night and decided to undergo hypnotic regression. The things he recalled in those regression sessions were what we would consider quite typical nowadays, at least mostly. As most people in this community know by now, no abduction story is the same as any other. Actually, they're all the same and yet completely unique in their own way. He was floated out of bed and through the wall of his bedroom and directly into a waiting spacecraft. He saw four different types of aliens that night. The first was a very small being who Whitley likened to a "robot". There was also a short, stocky type and then, the ever present thin, frail and weak one of the bunch. This to me is most likely a description of the greys as we have come to know them. Now, there is so much information on this abduction but bc I am doing a compilation of encounter stories in this book, and in the interest of saving time, I'm going to just give you the basics. Whitley did write a book which turned into a movie about his ordeal which you can find really anywhere books are sold.

Whitley said the sick and fragile looking alien had slanted, black eyes that were "mesmerizing" and all he said about the fourth type of alien was that it, too, had dark black eyes but that they were smaller and like little black buttons. These aliens ran numerous medical tests on him including the very feared yet ever present anal probe. They also inserted some sort of needle into his brain. When he was done recounting all of this, the hypnotherapist who was regressing him diagnosed him with temporal lobe epilepsy. They also took blood samples by making small incisions in his fingers as well. This "temporal lobe epilepsy" causes people to have hallucinations, very vivid ones at that. The doctor was alluding to the fact that Whitley had only hallucinated these things in his head and because he was so convinced in his head they had happened, he was able to recount them while under hypnotic regression. Whitley vehemently refutes that diagnosis and is adamant that his encounter was very real.

He went on to write a full book about this called "Communion". Whitley Streiber is now one of the most prominent and vocal researchers into UFO and extraterrestrial phenomena and mainly speaks and does most of his research on alien implants, abductions and hybrid programs. He warns of these things and has been telling people since his own experience about what's going on and how what happened to him isn't an isolated event. I tend to agree with him there and also, I believe he is a credible witness and professional person, again with much to lose by coming out with this. Especially the graphic detail he put into his novel Communion about the whole shocking and terrifying experience. Was this just a ploy to sell more books as some skeptics believe? I highly doubt it as he was doing perfectly fine selling his books and novels and even having so many of them made into movies, he didn't need the publicity. At least, in my own opinion.

CHAPTER 11
HILARY PORTER

Hillary Porter claims to have been abducted by aliens more times than she can count, she says the number could be as high as one hundred times! She claims these extraterrestrial visits started when she was just five years old and have been a constant in her life ever since. Hillary says, "I've been an alien abductee all my life. I didn't choose this life. I didn't ask for any of this, but it has been happening for as long as I can remember." Hillary comes off as credible to a lot of people, myself included, in part because she worked for the Ministry of Defense for a very long time. She is actually not the first woman I have found who has worked for some sort of military or government entity, especially in Britain, who has been abducted for most of their lives.

Hilary says she is keenly aware of what people say about her and that many if not most people don't even believe her but she doesn't care one bit because, just like many others who have been abducted, multiple times or even just once, she absolutely knows what happened to her and she knows she isn't crazy. The first encounter she can remember was when she was just five years old and playing in some tall grass in a field near her family home. She says, "Suddenly there was a reptilian alien in front of me. It had scaly skiing, black holes on the nose and a little mouth." She says, though this reptilian alien wasn't very tall, standing at somewhere close to five feet, she claims it was extremely strong. It suddenly reached out and grabbed her by her arms, pulling and dragging her across the field toward a disc shaped craft. It dragged her underneath the craft and she says there was a lift there which opened and she was put into it and then she was completely inside of and aboard the ship. She was in a room with little beings running all around with lots of bright lights and consoles all around her as well.

These reptilians were extremely rough with her, I feel almost sad as I have to keep reminding myself this was all happening to a very young and scared little girl. Hilary was stripped and tossed onto a sort of bed and she said they took a sharp instrument and were, "pressing it right the way up my body while I was screaming. I can't remember anything after that." Hillary has said that she believes she was actually abducted many times before this one, she just has no memory of it. She recalls many times when she would keep on disappearing seemingly into thin air from her own backyard, which was secured, and her frantic and terrified mother would find her a half a mile away with no memory or explanation as to how she got there. A two year old has very limited vocabulary and ability to express themselves and this is why I say all the time that very young children, toddlers especially, are prone to these abductions because they are truly helpless. Hilary said she believes it all started when she was a toddler.

Hilary has also said she was abducted near Cardiff, Wales, in the early 1970s. She said she was also abducted by a hexagonal looking spacecraft while "hanging out bunting" at a local charity event. Bunting is when someone stands or sits in public and performs for change or money from bystanders and passersby. She claims there was a top secret research plant inside a macaroni factory in which she worked in 1974, when an alien broke into it while she was there. When she went to work the next day, sections of the building were inaccessible and cordoned off. As well as a security guard who had "seen too much" and was also aware of the alien break in, was taken away for "mental health issues" and was allegedly never seen or heard from again. There are many things that go along with each abduction in Hilary's case. This is also quite common in a lot of people who are lifelong abductees. Extreme migraines, feeling extremely sick, sicker than you've ever been in your entire life, waking up with fresh scars and/or bruises and/or bloody marks or stains on your pajamas and bed sheets. These are just some of the common threads for each experiencer and what they also have to go through afterwards, as if the trauma of the abduction wasn't enough. These are tell-tale signs that something out of this world could be happening to you and the whole time you will just think you either had an intense nightmare or you won't remember it at all. Hilary's recountings of all of her abductions are very lengthy and not something I was able to cover in full here but it's a fascinating story and proves some of my own theories about why aliens choose the people they do to abduct or make contact with.

CHAPTER 12
CHERRY HINKLE

I know I've covered this case in one of my other books, Encounters With Evil Volume Two, but I am reluctant not to go over it again here because this book is specifically about extraterrestrial encounters and Cherry Hinkle's encounter story is one that both baffles and terrifies me. Also, not everyone reading this book will have read my other books, so I really felt compelled to include it here too.

In 1977 in Henderson, Nevada a woman named Cherry Hinkle lived alone with her thirteen year old son whose name was Marc. There were a lot of wooded and open areas there near their home at the time and on this particular day Marc and a friend decided to go and explore some of the nearby caves. They said they made their way to a circular chamber where they pretty much stumbled into an even deeper hole and when they shone their flashlights down there, the light barely penetrated the abyss. They decided to turn some branches into a sort of makeshift ladder and climb down into the darkness. Cherry Hinkle recounted to UFO Digest what her son had told her had happened that day. She reported, "The pit was roomy, with a short annex. Occasional debris littered the rocky floor, like a tin can or two, a battered teen magazine perched on a small outcrop of rock that served as a shelf. The boys explored the main cave, then turned their attention to the short tunnel or annex…[and] heard the sounds of voices and maybe the distant humming of machines. Intrigued by the thought of they were mining nearby, the boys went deeper into the tunnel. On the far end, they found a rusty metal door, and near the door a strange metal rod. The one-foot rod was lightweight and resembled aluminum, with a cap on one end and a few strange engravings on one side…Startled, the boys heard the sound or guttural harsh voices talking, and the certain sound of approaching footsteps. The boys became frightened by the strange vocalizations and high-tailed it to their makeshift ladder and headed up toward the cave entrance on the upper level. As they exited, they heard what sounded like the metal door opening, its old metal screeching. They crawled out the tunnel opening and ran away from the cave entrance. Thinking they were safe, they breathed a sigh of relief. Without a warning, they heard a loud threatening growl. Harry and Marc looked back at the cave entrance and to their horrified eyes; they watched as a very large greenish humanoid struggled to force his big body out of the narrow cave. The boys screamed and started running down the slope of the hill, running top speed! They didn't look back until they were near my back yard."

The boys seem to have brought proof with them out of the cave. Cherry said they showed her a rod-like object that they had taken with them. It had strange carvings and symbols all over it. It was smooth and metallic and unlike anything any of them had ever seen. She said she would have taken it to someone to have it looked at to see what kind of relic it was or if it was even anything that was known at all, but something strange that happened later that same night seemed to indicate that the strange cave creature wanted its object back. She explained what happened later on by saying, "It must have been around two in the morning when Marc shook me whispering harshly that someone is trying to get into his bedroom window. I hoped it was just a nightmare, or his nerves were still on edge. Quietly we slipped into his bedroom and listened to the sounds of scraping at the window edge! He was not mistaken—in the light of the moon I could make out the silhouette of the head and shoulders of a man. I was alone with my four kids, no husband to protect us, so I grabbed my flashlight; suddenly tossed the curtains open to face the man. There was a glare from the flashlight on the window, but past the glare I could clearly see a large head with ridges on the top, other ridges on his cheekbones, and the glow of golden eyes. Marc and I stood still, unmoving, both fear and shock kept us frozen. The Lizard Man didn't move either, his hand still poised in his attempt to pry the window open. His hand was large, with webbed, rough, gnarly looking fingers, with powerful claws. After a couple minutes, not seconds, but long agonized minutes with our hearts pounding I knew I had to do something. One hand still holding the flashlight beam on his face and my eyes still locked into those golden eyes, I fumbled around in the dark with my other hand, hoping to find something to use as a weapon if needed. He glanced at my hand, looked back into my eyes. He turned his head a little, as if he was asking a question, he slightly opened his lipless lips, displaying four of his pointed teeth, and suddenly he turned and ran off into the desert. Later in the morning, we decided the reason the Lizard Man was breaking in the house was to reclaim that metal rod. Marc and I hiked back to the cave and placed the strange rod beside the cave entrance."

I tried finding further information on this case but frustratingly, there was nothing else. No updates about how everyone is doing now, if they ever saw the creature again, if there had been other encounters or abductions. The internet has almost no more information, at least not that I could find, about what happened after this. I like to think that maybe nothing else happened and that Cherry and her son went on to live regular lives with no extraterrestrial interference. However, given what I now know about these particular extraterrestrial creatures, reptilians as we call them, I highly doubt that's the case. I guess we'll never know though.

CHAPTER 13
THE GROUSE MOUNTAIN INCIDENT

Let's talk a little about close encounters of the sixth kind, which is when a human being suffers a serious injury or dies as a result of a close encounter from one through five. I want to take time, very briefly, to explain what close encounters are and what each kind means. It'll be helpful for more than just this one incident going forward in this book. Close Encounters of the first kind is when sightings of a UFO comes close enough to a witness, typically within about five hundred feet, so that the structural details of the craft can be seen. In these encounters there's no interaction between the witness and the craft or from the craft to the environment. Close encounters of the second kind refer to sightings that are accompanied by physical effects on the environment, witnesses or other living beings or mechanical systems. These effects include but aren't limited to burns on the ground, broken branches, electrical interference, physiological effects like paralysis or heat, and physical or chemical traces like scorched vegetation. Of course those are all in the context of there having been a craft that landed at the spot or in the area, not just in general. The third kind refers to human observations of animate beings or extraterrestrials. Fourth refers to direct interaction with non-human entities. These interactions often but not always involve medical examinations, telepathic communication, missing time and profound psychological and/or physical after effects. Close encounters of the fourth kind are what are often referred to as "alien abductions" which usually involve the victims or witnesses being taken aboard the UFO or at least away from where they originally were during the moment of interactions. Close encounters of the fifth kind are usually the ones where the human being initiates contact with the extraterrestrial and many people use something akin to a CE-5 app to do so but there are many different ways in which to achieve this. However, it isn't always the human being doing the initiating and sometimes it's bilateral and mutual. In the official definition of what this is it says that the contact can either be initiated by the human or by the alien but I'm not sure I subscribe to that part of the definition because if the alien or extraterrestrial is initiating the contact then it would be, at least in my opinion, more akin to the fourth kind, normally but not always resulting in an abduction. There's also close encounters of the seventh kind, which are almost never discussed outside of the extraterrestrial and ufology communities, and that's when an alien and human mate to produce a hybrid species. There's an eighth kind too, but I am not going to open that can of worms because of many reasons but mainly because we won't be discussing any of those types of encounters here in this book. I encourage you all, as with anything else, to do your own research if you want more information on anything we talk about here. In our next encounter we will be discussing close encounters of the sixth kind and we will more than likely cover all of the above mentioned at some point in this book.

One of the most fascinating close encounter of the sixth kind, in my opinion, is the February 1954 Grouse Mountain incident. I chose this one specifically too, because the official determination of this particular incident directly goes against the actual evidence of what happened. The official determination is that this was a tragic accident due to a pilot error. Due to what's since been uncovered, particularly by UFO investigators, I'm shocked that the determination hasn't officially been changed to at least say something unknown or unclear happened, but also that most people do not know and have never heard about the Grouse Mountain incident. So, let's talk about it. On February 12, 1954 at approximately 10:30 in the morning Second Lieutenant Lamar Barlow was piloting his F86 Sabre jet over Grouse Mountain in British Columbia, Canada. Lamar had departed from McChord Air Force Base which is located across the border in Tacoma, Washington and the purpose of him being out that morning was nothing more than a standard instrument checking exercise. It's important to note here that the jet was fully armed but for this seemingly benign testing mission there should have been no reason he would have had to use any of the weapons on board or anything like that.

At first, the flight was normal and uneventful but it didn't take long for things to take a turn for the bizarre. A little after noon the control tower at McChord began to receive a "Madday" signal from Lamar's jet and he was informing them that the plane's compass was no longer working and because of that he was lost. According to the official records in this case, at exactly 12:06 pm, so an hour and thirty six minutes after he initially took off for this very benign and incredibly routine mission, it was determined that he was flying somewhere close to sixty miles north of Vancouver, Canada. Nine minutes later that distance dropped significantly and he was only fifteen miles north of the city, so he was making great progress at finding his way back, probably with help from the control center. However, he was quickly losing fuel by that time and preparations were made for him to make an emergency landing at Sea Island Airport in Vancouver. Before he could land though the communications with him completely ceased and no one knew where he was or when he would be land-ing, if he would be landing at all. Lieutenant Barlow and his plane were eventually recovered on a mountainside at twenty seven hundred feet altitude. The estimation was made that his plane had slammed head first into the side of the mountain while traveling at a speed of approximately seven hundred and fifty miles per hour! His body was found still strapped and buckled into his pilot seat, and the debris from the jet was scattered all over the place, in every direction.

Immediately there were national and international newspapers covering the tragic accident and within a few days the United States Air Force had made their official determination of what caused the crash public. They claimed he had seen "radar ghosts" and because of the loss of his navigational equipment he had become increasingly confused and disorientated. They said he had been much closer to Tacoma than they'd initially thought he was, and that by the time Grouse Mountain came into his view, he had no time to react and crashed into the mountainside. He was killed instantly. That sounds about right and makes almost perfect sense to someone who doesn't know any better and it seems that in this case the Air Force was betting on no one knowing any better or looking any deeper into what really happened here. Essentially they banked on people just taking their official word for it. However, some things didn't make sense to people, particularly why Lamar would have been going so fast while he was descending. The military dismissed these concerns and said it was nothing more than a lack of experience on Barlow's part but for some UFO investigators looking into the case, there were other things that didn't make sense about this case as well. For example, why was the jet carrying twenty four armed rockets simply to carry out a standard navigational exercise? The military counter argued that this was simply to mimic or reproduce the exact weight of the plane if it would be actually heading into combat, but the UFO investigators knew that this could have been done much easier without actually having the fully armed rockets on the craft at that time. Also, they thought sending such an inexperienced pilot up into the air with an armed plane as part of a standard exercise was simply implausible and was questionable to say the least.

Ultimately, just as they'd suspected previously with several cases throughout the years that they'd looked into, the UFO investigators asked whether Lamar Barlow had left Tacoma Air Force Base to carry out a training exercise, or if he'd really been sent up to investigate and intercept an anomalous object- with the so-called anomalous object being some sort of UFO. These suspicions grew even more with the fact that the entire area around the crash site was sealed off and protected with armed guards for several days following the incident. The official explanation for that was that it was done in order to ensure the scene wasn't contaminated and to make sure every last bit and piece of the wreckage was recovered- specifically the rockets themselves. However, it's unknown whether or not any of the rockets were ever fired or if they were all actually recovered. Reports of an alleged clean-up operation stated that "most" of the rockets were recovered, but not all of them. Obviously there were a lot of people at that point that refused to accept the official explanation for Lamar's death and the crash itself. There was just too much about it that didn't make any sense. Because of those doubts the questions as to what he was really doing up there and whether or not he had been trying to intercept a UFO persist.

Many of the investigators involved wondered if he was instructed to use deadly force and whatever else it would take to get the anomalous object or objects out of the sky. Had it been that potential use of deadly force which caused his death? There was a lot more at play here too that came into question and didn't make much sense given the official military explanation for the tragic crash. For example, there were strange radar echoes heard that day that have never been explained, and there's also been no explanation, official or otherwise, as to what had caused his navigational equipment to fail in the first place. In light of these remaining questions it's interesting to note here that many pilots who have encountered UFOs while in the air, including military, private and commercial, have often reported having problems with their navigations and communications equipment, saying it was almost as though they'd been intentionally jammed. Another interesting fact here is that, at the time of the Grouse Mountain Incident, the military often used the term "phantom radar echoes" as the overall explanation for any kind of aerial anomaly.

A UFO researcher named Gord Heath came to his own potential explanation as to what happened to Lamar Barlow that morning at Grouse Mountain and also about what had caused his navigation and communication equipment to fail in the first place. He said it was highly strange and unusual that a pilot would have been allowed to stray so far off course in the first place and that it was standard practice for the control tower to alert the pilot in those circumstances. Why should it have been any different in this case? Particularly when you think about the fact that Barlow had crossed the border into another country he had strayed so far away, because he wasn't initially supposed to be in Canada. Remember that according to the official report, the first time the control tower was aware there was even a problem was when Lamar began issuing his Madday calls following the loss of his navigational equipment. Think about it though- if he were out there on an interception mission like many people believe he was, then the control tower would have had no reason to worry or wonder about why he had gone so far off course because they would have known what he was doing up there. Gord Heath said about all of this and his own conclusions, "Which makes more sense? The radar operators ignored the jet flying off into Canadian airspace until the pilot suddenly realizes he has only thirty minutes of fuel and has no clue about his position OR the radar operators guided the pilot in pursuit of a UFO into Canadian airspace, beyond the farthest distance to return to base thinking the pilot would be able to land safely at Vancouver?" Many other UFO researchers and enthusiasts agreed with Heath's statement but there was a witness who eventually came forward and provided information that you would think would only have come from a major Hollywood blockbuster movie. A twist of epic proportions.

This witness was a six year old girl who was returning to school after going home for her lunch break at the time and her name was Robin McPherson. Robin told newspaper reporters that she watched as a jet-plane had narrowly just missed a ski lift when she first noticed it. She said the plane was "awful low" and "came out of the clouds traveling very fast." She went on to tell reporters, "Then it sort of zoomed up and went in the trees on the side of the mountain. I didn't hear any noise like a bang." To add to all the confusion and intrigue in this case, in that same newspaper article a military spokesperson who most people didn't think had gotten permission to do so, questioned why Barlow had not "bailed out" of the plane when he saw it was about to crash into the side of the mountain. This official stated it was standard practice to do so and said that Lamar was, "flying as blind as a bat!" However, despite all of this new evidence and all of those new and interesting statements, the military seemed determined to make sure that no one blamed anyone except Barlow and only Barlow for the crash that day. Of course there's been no evidence put forth that proves there ever was a UFO in the skies that day or that Barlow had been sent up to intercept it at all. The rumors still persist to this day though and honestly this is far from the only time the death of a military pilot happened under such bizarre and seemingly inexplicable, questionable circumstances. In fact, just months before the Grouse Mountain Incident happened, a similar incident unfolded and it once again happened along the American-Canadian border. It was several hundred miles to the east in the Soo Locks area of Lake Superior in Michigan.

CHAPTER 14
THE CUNNINGHAM/LOVETTE INCIDENT

A few years after the Grouse Mountain Incident took place, in March of 1956, another blood-curdling event happened regarding two more military personnel. According to the official report Sergeant Johnathan Lovette and Mayor William Cunningham were at the White Sands missile testing grounds near Holloman Air Force Base, in New Mexico's Tularosa Basin, and they were there looking for rocket debris. During their search Sergeant Lovette decided to go off on his own to search the edge of a small sand dune somewhat nearby. For just a moment he disappeared from Mayor Cunningham's sight and within seconds he heard a blood-curdling, terrifying scream coming from where he had just seen his friend. Immediately Cunningham thought that Lovette had been bitten by a snake or something like that and he ran over to the edge of the sand dune to see if he could help and what was going on but he was greeted with a sight that he couldn't quite wrap his head around. He looked over and saw a large, shiny silver disc hovering over the ground about twenty feet away from where he was standing. There was an opening in the object and from it something tentacle-like was reaching down out of it. He followed the tentacle from the top where it was coming from the opening in the craft to where it was on the ground and saw that it was wrapped around Lovette's leg! Lovette, during all of this, was screaming in terror and probably pain too, as Cunningham helplessly watched on in fear, unable to move or do anything to help his friend. Finally and within just a few seconds, the thing dragged Lovette towards it and he disappeared completely into the opening. As soon as he was inside and the opening closed, the disc shaped shiny silver craft shot off into the air and disappeared.

It took a few minutes for Cunningham to come to his senses but once he did he ran back to the military Jeep and radioed back to base and told them what had just transpired. He was terrified and still really couldn't believe what had just happened. By the time several military units arrived in response to that distress call, Cunningham was in a complete state of shock. He was taken to a military hospital where he was kept under twenty four hour observation. While there in the hospital he was questioned several times about what had actually transpired between him and Lovette on the day in question, and each and every time he told them the exact same thing he had been telling them from the beginning, which was the same exact thing he had told them in the initial distress call he placed immediately after the incident occurred. The same thing I've just repeated to all of you. His official recounting of events according to the records I found was that he had seen Lovette dragged aboard a flying saucer by a large tentacle-like appendage and then the craft had disappeared into the sky very quickly afterward. An interesting fact here too is that, at least according to the official report, the radar system at the base had detected an anomalous object in the same region where Lovette had disappeared from, and at the same time. This anomalous object had simply vanished off the radar into nothingness at the exact same time Cunningham had reported the craft had taken off and disappeared with Lovette inside of it.

Of course the military sent many search units out into that region and they all combed over the area for three whole days. Eventually they discovered Lovette's naked corpse approximately ten miles away from where he had last been seen alive but being dragged into a spaceship by Cunningham. It was estimated that his body had been left out in the elements anywhere from twelve to twenty four hours. This means there were approximately forty eight hours when his body was unaccounted for and his where-abouts were otherwise unknown. His body was eventually returned to base and an autopsy was performed but it did nothing to help matters and only ended up producing more questions and no more answers. Though his body had been completely and totally mutilated, it had been done with great care and precision. There were very similar cuts and injuries that we have now come to see a lot in the cattle mutilation cases. For example, a part of his lower jaw had been precisely cut away and his tongue had been surgically removed from his mouth. His eyes and also, somewhat even more bizarrely, his anus had also been completely and totally removed. The latter had been described as having been taken out, "as if it were a plug or cork-stop."

It was determined that whoever, or in this case probably what-ever, had inflicted these grotesque injuries most definitely had extremely advanced surgical and medical knowledge, not to mention very well honed skills. The most unsettling thing for me and for many people who are familiar with this particular case, and this is also something we would come to see all the time in the cattle mutilation cases in the following decades, is the fact that he had been completely exsanguinated. Meaning, every drop of blood was drained from his body, and even though the cattle mutilations wouldn't start to become "a thing" until the early 1960s, if you know about and are familiar with them then you will know that this happens ninety nine percent of the time in each and every one of those cases. To add to the mystery of this already very confusing and macabre case, was the fact that the autopsy found no sign of vascular collapse. This is important because someone who had bled to death like Lovette was thought to have done would have definitely had this vascular collapse. Somehow, and this is wild, Cunningham's superiors accused him of murdering Lovette, but they obviously had no evidence. Where would he have stashed the body during the forty eight hours Lovette was still alive somewhere before he was mutilated? Also, he was under hospital supervision, constant for all twenty four hours of the day and never without someone's eyes on him, when the body was found and he would have had to have moved it from wherever he had been keeping it and put it where it was found, which as you can already tell would have been impossible. Due to lack of evidence, but not lack of suspicion, he was released without ever being charged with anything in this case.

A report of this incident from Project Grudge, simply titled Report 13, brought another interesting element to this case that I wanted to mention here before we move on. Two people came forward saying that they had been asked to analyze a document for the US military and this is actually the report where most of the public information on this case comes from. The people were two men, one named William Cooper who was only called a researcher and the other was Captain William English, who was a former Green Beret. Cooper said he had seen an annotated version of the report sometime in the early 1970s while English said that he looked into it several years later while he was assigned to the United States security service based out of Royal Air Force Base in Chicksands, England. Both of these men had given their reports separately and independently of one another and neither had knowledge of the other man or what he said or even that anyone else had looked into the case at all, and yet both of them recalled identical versions of the events. Another interesting thing to note here is that Report 13 no longer officially exists, and all of the other reports in Project Grudge, so reports 1-12 and then 14 and upward, are available in the public domain. Every single report, except for Report 13. Now if that isn't suspicious then I don't know what is!

CHAPTER 15
CISCO GROVE

On September 4,1964 a twenty eight year old man named Donald Shrum and some of his friends went bow hunting in Cisco Grove, Placer County, California and somehow and at some point Donald had become separated from his group. It was almost fully dark outside and the men were having this adventure in the middle of the woods, so he decided to just hunker down inside of a tree for the night. He figured he would just catch up with his friends the following morning so they could continue on their adventure. He started drifting from half sleep to half awake daydreams and back again and was having a very hard time either falling asleep or staying awake. Suddenly though he was snapped out of it when he saw a dazzling and bright white light zigzagging through the darkness and the trees surrounding him. At first he thought it was a helicopter and although he couldn't imagine why one would be there just then, in that place at that time, he wasn't scared or worried about it. However, once the mysterious light started slowly coming towards him and then as it started hovering in the sky almost directly above the tree he was trying to sleep in, his feelings changed. He was scared and didn't know what was happening but because of how silent everything was, including the light or whatever it was attached to. He knew for sure it wasn't a helicopter of any kind. He tried his best to stay still and silent, hoping that whatever was piloting the craft attached to the light, which he knew had to be there but couldn't yet see, wouldn't notice that he was there. However, he quickly realized that whatever it was had noticed him and when he looked down onto the ground below the tree he had been resting in, he saw three strange looking beings approaching him. He described two of the beings as humanoid in general shape but the third one he would explain looked like some sort of outlandish and bizarre robot. The beings started to shake the tree ferociously and with great force, as the terrified Donald tried his best to hold on and to keep his eyes on the creatures below. He knew right away that they were trying to dislodge him from where he was and get him to drop to the ground. As he watched, the "robot" started sputtering something that looked like white steam from its mouth, and then Donald fell fast and deeply asleep.

He woke up a few minutes later and realized the creatures were still trying to get him out of the tree and hadn't succeeded yet, despite having been successful at knocking him unconscious for a little while. He didn't know what to do and really didn't have much recourse against this strange and bizarre attack and so he did the only thing he could think to do at the time, which was drop lit matches on top of them. This only caused them to back up a bit, for a few seconds, before they went right back to their efforts at getting him out of the tree. He then remembered he had a weapon on him and started shooting at them with his bow. He noticed that the arrows he was shooting at them caused sparks to shoot out of the top of the robot-looking entity's head as they hit and bounced off of it. As time passed, more and more of the robot creatures appeared and the humanoid looking entities were trying unsuccessfully to crawl up the tree towards him. Donald said he shot arrows at them until he didn't have any more left and then he just threw anything he had on him or near him that he could think of, in the hopes of getting them to leave him alone. There was a point when he was gassed again by the white mist stuff from the robot's mouth but when he snapped out of it once again he saw that the creatures were still desperately trying to get to him. This went on until the sun started to rise and then they just stopped trying to get to him and left him alone. Later on, his companions had asked him if he had seen the strange lights in the sky shooting and zipping around all night. They wholeheartedly believed Donald's story and said it wasn't something he would lie about and he wasn't known to be a fibber.

I can't even imagine how terrified Donald must have been while in that tree and basically under siege by these bizarre creatures. Not to mention, with all of the research I've done into encounters and abductions with extraterrestrial creatures, if I were him I would have been almost non-stop worrying about that stuff that emitted from the one being that knocked me out. What was that and does it have any lasting effects or dire consequences? This encounter really got to me. I kept getting goosebumps as I went through this information and I also just kept wondering what would have happened to and become of him had he not had the presence of mind in the first place to decide to sleep IN the tree. What if he had decided to sleep under it instead? They would have had full access to him and who knows what their intentions were.

CHAPTER 16
TOSSEY/BEGAY

On November 2, 1967 near a town called Ririe, Idaho, two Native American men named Guy Tossie and Will Begay were driving south on Highway 26 when they had their harrowing almost abduction encounter. The men saw a glowing, dome shaped object appear in front of their vehicle in a flash of light. It was about eight feet wide and there were humanoid entities of some sort inside of the dome, which was transparent. They looked at everything around them in shock and some astonishment and their car suddenly came to a stop, stalling out as the engine died for no reason, leaving them with no way to get away from whatever was unfolding before them. One of the hinges on the bizarre looking dome shaped craft opened up, and then one of the entities that had been inside of it exited and floated itself down to the ground. It had completely defied gravity and the witnesses saw that it was approximately three feet tall, had large black eyes and a bulbous head. They were more than a little terrified, obviously. The creature then walked confidently right up to the car and let itself inside with them, taking a seat right behind the steering wheel and pushing whoever was driving over to the side and out of the way so that it could sit there instead.

Once the being was behind the wheel, the car suddenly started up again and it began to drive very slowly right towards the craft it had just come from as the other two beings inside looked on and watched. The craft was hovering about five feet above the ground and suddenly the vehicle veered off to the side of the road and into a large wheat field. The dome shaped object/craft started slowly following it, presumably trying to get into a position of hovering over the vehicle with the men and the other entity inside of it. When the car finally came to an abrupt stop in the field, Guy made a break for it and opened the door, running out into the night and shouting for help. He headed for a farmhouse he could see nearby. The farmhouse was owned by a local man named Willard Hammon. The UFO followed Guy almost the entire way but once he actually reached Willard's house, the craft backed off and started heading back into the field to where the car was. All the while, Will Begay was still in the car with the being who was still behind the wheel. The being turned to look at him and started to "curse him out" or so he thought because that's what the barrage of angry sounding, bird-like noises it let out towards him sounded like. It then stormed out of the car, floated back up into the craft and then the craft zigzagged off into the night sky.

Guy brought the farmer back to Will, who was astonished and traumatized, still sitting in the exact same spot in the vehicle, almost unblinking and unmoving, not knowing what to do next. Will and Guy filed a police report and at first the authorities didn't take what they had to say seriously at all. However, reports from other witnesses began to pour into the station of people saying they had seen strange lights in the sky and that many of them had livestock that had been acting bizarrely in response to the lights and possibly something else, something connected to it. Both of our witnesses insist to this day that those were aliens and that they were trying to abduct them. They believe that Guy running to go and get help more than likely saved them from whatever their fate otherwise would have been had the entities been successful. This is another one where I just cannot imagine how in the world I would react to something like this and in all the information that I had about this case, I haven't found anything about what the farmer, Willard Hammon, thought about it all or if he saw anything.

CHAPTER 17
LYDIA MOREL

This one was very short and there was almost no information about it but it was too bizarre for me to pass up and falls under the "almost abducted" title as far as extraterrestrial encounters go. This happens a lot more than most people think and I believe her story and what happened to her are just as important as the more well-known cases that are discussed almost constantly in the extraterrestrial and ufology communities.

In 1973 a masseuse at the Swedish Sauna in Manchester, England named Lyndia Morel had finished up a late shift on the night of November 2, and she was driving home to the nearby town of Goffstown, at around 2:45 in the morning. Her house in Goffstown was about eight miles from her job in Manchester so it wasn't a very long way for her to have to travel, especially not at that late hour. As she drove, she kept on seeing an intermittent flash of light that switched colors between yellow, red, blue and green, which she said she thought was an aircraft or a planet. Eventually though she saw it closer and noticed it was a very large and glowing orb covered in hexagonal shapes. She described it as being "like a honeycomb" and she said once it got very close to her, her head had been invaded by some sort of high pitched squealing sound. She noticed she couldn't remove her hands from the steering wheel, no matter how hard she tried. Her vehicle began to move itself towards the glowing object, in which she could see, "a smallish humanoid figure standing behind a console of some sort" inside of the object. She said it was trying to send her a telepathic message, telling her to calm down and not to be afraid. Suddenly Lyndia felt warm and calm, and she was overwhelmed by a sleepiness she couldn't resist. However, she somehow snapped out of whatever mind- control the entities were attempting, and the calm that had suddenly washed over dissolved just as quickly as it had overwhelmed her. Lydia managed to regain control of her vehicle and she veered off the course she was on, speeding towards a nearby house. She made it to the house, stopped the car, got out and ran to the residence, pounding on the door even as the whole time the UFO hovered nearby. It was watching her and the high pitched squealing was still assaulting her ears. The residents of the house opened the door and saw this terrified woman standing out there, looking desperately and pleading with them for help, they called the police and let her come inside. As soon as she stepped foot inside of the house, the craft shot off into the sky and disappeared. There's no more information out there about what happened to Lydia after that but more than likely she made it home that night and the cops either believed her or didn't. This is just the kind of lesser known case that makes me terrified of all the others out there, where people are too afraid to come forward with their experiences.

CHAPTER 18
FILIBERTO CARDENAS

In 1979 in Hialeah, Florida in the United States, a man named Filiberto Cardenas and his wife were out driving from place to place to try and get a pig for a pig roast the following weekend. They were having a hard time finding what they were looking for. By the time they were ready to call it quits it had become dark outside and they got lost while trying to find their way back. They accidentally turned down a dark and lonely stretch of rural road and while driving, their car stalled out and the engine, for seemingly no reason, wouldn't turn over. They got out of the car and thoroughly checked their vehicle but they couldn't seem to find anything wrong with it. Suddenly, as they were standing there trying to figure out what was going on and how they were going to get out of there and back home, a very loud and terrible sound, which they both likened to thousands of hives of buzzing bees, filled the air around them. It completely invaded not only their ears but their senses as well. They quickly got back into their car and as they were just sitting there wondering what in the world was going on and what they should do next, the car started vibrating and shaking as though there were a sudden earthquake. All around them the color of red and purple lights danced through the trees and as his wife screamed in what I'm sure was a mix between terror and sheer panic, Filiberto himself was paralyzed and lifted out of his seat by some unseen force.

Filiberto later reported that when he had lost consciousness and when he woke again he was still paralyzed but no longer in his car. He said he was in a room with humanoid beings wearing helmets all around him and that the room itself was "shiny." The beings then all started to speak to each other all at once, almost excitedly, and he explained the language these beings spoke to each other was reminiscent of German- or so he thought. What happened next isn't anything out of the ordinary if you're familiar with abductions and how some of them tend to work sometimes. Filiberto was staring at a giant screen on the wall in front of him that was showing images flashing quickly before him, one after the other. He said that in those scenes there were many important points in the Earth's history but that he couldn't remember enough and the images flew past one another so quickly, and so there's never been any further detail as to what these images really entailed. These quick flashes of images weren't just of the planet's past but of what he understood to be the future as well.

Once the images were done flashing there before him, he was brought to a much smaller craft that detached from a larger one he hadn't even realized at first he'd been sitting in. This smaller craft then went shooting off towards what he thought looked very much like a beach. The craft seemed to almost glide over the sand very quickly and it easily crashed into and submerged itself deep into the ocean. Filiberto said the ship then glided slowly through a series of long, underwater tunnels which all seemed to be brightly lit by some sort of bioluminescence. It passed through those tunnels and eventually came to an abrupt stop in some dry area within the deep blue sea. Yes, he was in a dry area inside of a very wet and very vast ocean. He described it as "a sort of cavern or air pocket" and the first thing he noticed were symbols of what looked like snakes were drawn all over the walls of the area. Our witness/victim was then taken out of that ship and made to sit on a large rock and after he sat there in fear and awe for several moments, a human man came out of one of the other tunnels and welcomed him.

The man seemed friendly and explained to Filiberto that he was from Earth but that he worked with the aliens. The man took him by the hand and walked with him until they entered a large city of sorts, only it was underground and inside of the ocean. He was shown and told many prophecies while he was there but he has no memory of what he saw in the city or what was told to him and most of what he does remember only came back after some time and even then only in bits and pieces. Some of the prophecies Filiberto said he'd been shown that night were the election of President Ronald Reagan in 1980, the earthquake in Mexico City in 1985, the assassination of Anwar Sadat in 1981- he was the president of Egypt at the time he was killed, and the demonstration by Chinese students in Tiananmen Square in 1989. He also predicted the Gulf War, which started in 1990 between Iran and Saddam Hussein and the United States. He told some of the predictions to his closest friends and family but he didn't publicly speak about them and it's hard to find corroboration of the fact that he predicted these things at all, but like with everything else I work on in this community, I like to keep an open mind and give people the benefit of the doubt because, especially at the time this is all said to have happened, someone like Filiberto would have had much more to lose than he had to gain by talking about these experiences publicly at all and there's really no reason for him to have made it all up.

CHAPTER 19
BETTY LUCA

Our next encounter story dates all the way back to 1950 and was reported by a woman named Betty Andreason Luca. Betty was a homemaker and housewife, mother and grandmother as well. The memory of what happened to her came back when she had undergone hypnosis and the incident had originally taken place when she was only a child. She remembered being in her childhood home on an evening just like any but the details of exactly what she'd been doing when this all happened are nonexistent, or at least I couldn't find them, but that should have no bearing on the encounter at all anyway. Betty says she was suddenly taken aboard and flown away on what she described as "a wheel-like vehicle" that went speeding off into the night and then crashed into a very large body of water. It had been dark out when this all happened so she really couldn't see much of what was going on, not that she would have understood much of it if she could. Betty would later say that the speed of the vehicle was unlike and faster than anything she'd ever seen or ridden inside of before. This happened in 1950 and they didn't even have horsepower in their vehicles at that time but even still, she'd described it as much faster than anything we have resembling vehicles here on Earth on the ground.

As the craft approached the water Betty was frightened. That was mainly because it showed no signs of stopping or even just slowing down, and with the superhuman speed at which it was traveling, she knew that a fast and probably deadly crash was imminent. She thought for sure that she and whoever else was on board with her, at that time she couldn't see anyone or anything else, would die and she braced herself for impact. However, instead of the ship crashing and Betty dying, the vehicle, still moving very quickly, smoothly went down into the depths of the water and continued submerging who knows how far down. It all happened so fast that Betty was obviously and understandably terrified and very confused by the whole experience, especially remembering that she was only a very young child at the time this all took place. The craft continued down into the depths of the water without so much as a hiccup and Betty remembered it hardly even hesitated as it did all of this.The craft was still moving at the exact same extremely high rate of speed as it had been when she was first taken into it and it hadn't slowed down a bit. It continued to travel in this way and at this rate of speed while underwater, obviously set on a specific destination. It seemed to have been on some kind of autopilot, at least as far as Betty was aware at the time. Eventually and after traveling for what seemed like a very long time, despite the desperately fast speed, the vehicle came to a gigantic, dome-shaped facility. Betty refers to this facility as a base of some sort.

She first saw a bunch of people, presumably other human beings, inside of what looked like glass containers. The containers were just hanging in the air through what seemed to be some sort of suspended animation or something. With the way gravity and physics work here on this planet, the way these "pods" were just hanging there out of thin air shouldn't have been possible at all-yet there they were. The people in the containers were just hovering there, in space and time, as though they'd been frozen in place, in mid-air, inside of strange capsules. Betty said she thought they were in sets and she referred to them in many interviews as "museums of time." She said she thought of that name for them because there were hundreds or possibly even thousands of those people, all of them wearing clothing reminiscent of one time period or another throughout hundreds of years of history. She thought there could have been enough people there, from enough different time periods, to cover the beginning of time until that moment. For each time period the people wearing that era of clothing all had their glass containers in clusters with one another. There was an almost limitless number of rows of people and they were of all different ages and races, as well as rows of all different kinds of animals, both extinct at the time Betty experienced this and living at that time as well.

Betty said she'd sat there for just a few minutes taking in this strange sight and then suddenly the ship started up again and immediately resumed its incredibly fast speed, taking her home and leaving her there to forget the entire incident for decades. Thirty years later, in 1980, Betty started to have insanely vivid nightmares that tormented and terrified her and she was finally convinced that she needed to undergo hypnosis. She's been met with a lot of scorn and ridicule since going public with her story but most people think that's because this isn't the only strange experience Betty had publicly announced she'd gone through. She claimed to have met what she called "Servants of Jesus" in the form of angelic aliens whom she claims to have encountered a few times as well, but the details are almost non-existent for those encounters as well. It is worth mentioning here that someone else came forward with a similar report to Betty's, from around the same time and in the same area, and as many of us already know, these types of things aren't uncommon when it comes to UAPs-Underwater Abduction Phenomenon.

CHAPTER 20
THE NEIGHBORS

In the fall of 2010 a man who we will call Mark was living in what he described as a "run down" apartment complex in NYC. He had a roommate who traveled a lot for work and he was left alone in the apartment for a majority of the time he lived there. Mark explained that the turnover rate was high in the complex because of how much of a dump it was, and so he was used to seeing people moving in and out all the time. It was for that reason when he saw that someone new had moved into the apartment across from him he didn't think anything of it at first. However, he was about to experience some real high strangeness regarding the people who moved in across the hall from him very soon after they took up residence there. The new tenant, whose name neither Mark nor anyone else ever really learned, will be called "Jeff" for the purposes of this story and it didn't take long for Mark to notice that Jeff was an eccentric and a recluse, which honestly isn't too odd in the city nowadays and probably wasn't the epitome of strangeness fifteen years ago either. Jeff was almost never seen by anyone else in the building and according to Mark he almost never left his run down apartment. As far as the other neighbors were concerned, the man never exchanged pleasantries or spoke at all to any of the other people in the building either, even when they would on the rare occasion see him and try to be friendly or strike up mundane conversation. Jeff was said to either very quickly leave the area without explanation and without ever engaging any of the conversations being aimed at him. He would also sometimes just stop and stand perfectly still while being spoken to, staring off into space and barely even breathing until the other person stopped talking. Then Jeff would run off, again without responding at all to whatever had been said to him at the time. Jeff left the television on in his apartment all hours of the day and night and most of the time it was loud, and Mark also noticed the endless procession of delivery people going up to the door to bring him his meals. This was odd in and of itself because this was a very poor neighborhood and if the man never left his house then it left Mark wondering how he made his money that he was able to afford all that expensive take out for every meal, every day. Though the apartment was run down and somewhat dreadful, Mark said that it was still in the heart of New York City and he wondered how Jeff was able to afford to live there when all he seemed to do was sit around all day listening to the tv and ordering take out for himself.

Not long after he moved in, it seemed like Jeff had someone move in with him as well and Mark described her as an "Asian looking" woman who was young and every single bit as odd and weird as Jeff was. One day he met the woman in the hallway and said hello to her. She just stopped short in her tracks and stared straight at him, unblinkingly. When he repeated his hello she merely responded, in a strange and somewhat robotic tone- possibly a mock Asian accent "I stay here" as she pointed to the door of Jeff's apartment. Mark didn't know what else to do and so he just walked away and went about his business with a polite nod. When he turned around he saw that the woman was still standing perfectly still and staring at him, watching him walk away, unblinkingly, before turning and walking into Jeff's apartment. She slammed the door loudly behind her but he figured maybe they were just your typical unfriendly New Yorkers. That sentiment would quickly change as he realized that maybe something more sinister was going on with his new neighbors after all.

A few weeks after the initial encounter with the woman, Mark's roommate came back from another out of town business trip and said he had some interesting news about their new neighbors from an encounter a friend of his who worked delivering pizza had with the mysterious couple a few weeks earlier. The roommate said that his friend told him that when Jeff answered the door he grabbed the pizza and slammed the money into the guy's hands, trying to then slam the door shut in his face without saying a word. The guy took a step forward to thank him for the generous tip but said that it was like Jeff was trying very hard not to let the delivery guy see into the very dark apartment. Suddenly the Asian looking woman came out of the darkness, out of nowhere, and when she saw the delivery guy at the door she stopped short, turned and ran back out of sight. The two men, meaning Mark and his roommate, tried to figure out why the couple was so weird. They speculated as to what they could possibly be hiding or doing in the apartment but they couldn't come up with anything and so they almost forgot about it or at the very least didn't trouble themselves with thinking about it anymore.

One night Mark was coming home from going out to dinner with some friends in the city and he just happened to run into Jeff and the woman in the hallway as they were heading into their apartments at the same time. Mark said he said hello but must've startled the couple because the woman dropped a whole bag of groceries onto the floor in response to his cheerful hello. He said every single item that was in the bag and that had fallen to the floor was canned meat and when he apologized and tried to help the strange woman pick it all up, Jeff practically commanded him, in a very agitated and angry voice, to "back up. Leave it alone. Leave it!" He said Jeff had practically growled those things at him. He stopped and looked up, as Jeff started muttering some sort of apology, and when he did he saw that Jeff's eyes were different than they had been just seconds before or at any other time he remembered seeing him- or the woman because her eyes had changed as well. While the woman usually had gorgeous and somewhat a-typical eyes, for an Asian woman at least, green eyes and Jeff's eyes had been a beautiful and clear sky blue color. They both had all black eyes at that moment in the hallway. Their eyes had no whites left in them and no color, and reminded Mark of the predatory eyes of a shark. It startled our witness to the point that he physically recoiled in horror and tried to suppress the loud gasp that came out of his mouth. He started backing away towards his apartment's door while stuttering out an apology and trying not to look anywhere but at the ground. He couldn't help but look up though, as he was backing away, and by the time he reached his door- he had backed up into it- both Jeff's and the woman's eyes had morphed right before his eyes back to their normal- albeit unusual- colors.

The couple rushed into their apartment so quickly that they left a lot of the canned meat they had dropped right there in the hallway on the ground. They slammed their door loudly behind them and only then did Mark feel safe enough to turn his back and go into his apartment. He was thinking about it and decided he should at least pick up the rest of their groceries for them, feeling less scared and somewhat bad about the whole interaction to begin with. I just want to say that as human beings we have a tendency to do this and I think it really plays well into the advantage of entities that mean us harm or that aren't from this realm or dimension as they probably know us well enough to know that we will absolutely do everything we can to try and talk some sense into ourselves and convince ourselves that we didn't in fact see what we just know we saw, even if only moments earlier. Our minds work in such a way that if something is too terrifying or too abnormal, we tend to make every effort we can, even leaning into the preposterous, to convince ourselves that everything is just fine and perfectly normal when we know deep down inside it isn't. I am sure this is what happened to our witness when only moments later he regretted the whole encounter and instead of being scared out of his mind he decided to go out and pick up that meat for the strange couple- despite what he had just witnessed with his own eyes only moments earlier. He didn't even have the chance to close his door yet before he decided to go pick the cans of meat up off the floor but when he turned around, they were all gone already.

Obviously Mark was really unsettled because not only had he just seen what he did, he knew that the cans of meat were there one moment and gone the very next. He didn't understand what could possibly have been going on but did the best he could to put it out of his mind. He made plans for that November, so about a month or two later, to go and spend Thanksgiving with some friends so that he wouldn't be home for about a week. When he got home he immediately realized that the television wasn't on all the time anymore, nor was it blaring when it was, in Jeff's apartment. He also noticed very quickly that the endless procession of delivery drivers had ceased altogether. He secretly hoped that Jeff and the lady had moved out and when he talked to the landlord it turned out he got his wish. The landlord complained that they had moved out in the middle of the night and bailed on the rent that they owed. It wasn't quite over just yet though and Mark said that after Jeff moved out, he began having some strange and bizarre psychological issues or effects. He started feeling claustrophobic in his apartment, which he had never felt before and he didn't understand where it was coming from. Not only that but he had a strange aversion to meat as well. Never having been a vegetarian before nor had he ever considered it even, he found that he was absolutely repulsed by the thought of meat and couldn't be near it without vomiting. He tried nibbling on some chicken but became sick for days and says that he still isn't able to eat meat without being sick for days or even weeks afterwards.

Interestingly enough, Mark has convinced himself that Jeff and the woman weren't only entities that weren't human, but that they had either purposely cursed him or he had inadvertently been cursed, when he looked directly into their black eyes during the hallway encounter. Shortly after all of this happened, a little after the new year, he moved to Boston and tried to put the whole ordeal behind him. He was doing well but then he ran into a paranormal investigator and David Weatherly- known by many for his books on the black eyed kid phenomenon- while at a conference of some sort and he ended up telling them his story. David believed in it so much that he ended up putting it in his book, called "Strange Intruders" but honestly, at least in my opinion, this one is very hard to categorize because there's still so many unknowns to it. Were they extraterrestrials or something different altogether? Were they regular human beings who were just odd? But, if you believe that then you can't believe Mark's whole story because then how would their eyes have changed like that right before his eyes? I believe Mark and I believe in his story, mainly because I know for a fact things like this do happen but that most of the time it's a one off and doesn't have such intense consequences as Mark's experiences with these people had. The forced vegetarianism, the crippling claustrophobia- but then, what were they? If they were aliens then what kind and why are they here? Where did they go and what does that mean for the black eyed kid phenomenon? There's just too many open ended questions here for me to be able to make even an educated guess at what in the world this guy experienced but I will say it was paranormal or at the very least otherworldly in nature. After all, this encounter and the next one I am about to share with you I obtained from the National UFO Reporting Center or NUFON's archived files.

CHAPTER 21

THE IDES OF MARCH SIGHTINGS/THE PHOENIX LIGHTS

On March 15, 1995 the NUFORC started to receive tons of calls across dozens of states from witnesses reporting that they had seen or were seeing a bright object flying all across the night sky. This is called "The Ides of March Sightings" and the first of them to be reported to NUFORC was reported by two men in Florida who described the light as "luminous, white and disc shaped." Subsequent descriptions varied though and someone from Tennessee called and said that to him it looked more like "a blue-green cloud of light" that emitted sparks before vanishing into the night sky. A sergeant from the Missouri State Highway Patrol witnessed the event too and he reported it being a green light that turned yellow and then went out "like a light being switched off." That witness also explained that so many people were calling the local 911 in the area and reporting to the dispatchers that they were all seeing the same exact thing as what he had just described with one of those callers saying that his cellphone and car radio both died when the UFO got too close to the vehicle. It was 1995 and this more than likely would have meant his car phone, as I don't think cellular phones were very popular back then, if they existed at all. Either way, it's actually very common for UFOs to interfere with vehicles and other technology just like what was described here. There were still other reports that came in of what was thought to be the same object from Virginia, West Virginia and Missouri, just to name a few other places. The official report summarized the event very briefly by saying, "In summary, it appears as though one or more egg shaped objects, radiating intensely bright green, blue-green and yellow light, periodically spewing out a cloud of sparks, streaked over at least seven states, stopping from time to time, and the whole event occurred in a matter of minutes." When you have multiple witnesses across multiple states and some of those witnesses are police officers and other somewhat respected members of society, I ask again and with even more fervor- why the hell did no one at all address what this was in the paper or on the news the next day? Probably because our government wanted it swept under the rug like it does with most things. "Allegedly."

I think for the most part many people have heard about The Phoenix Lights before at some point in their lives. In March of 1997 it was Arizona that played host to an event that NUFORC called "perhaps the most dramatic UFO sighting that's been reported in many years." Dozens of people from all over the state called in to the hotline and reported that they were seeing a group of white or red lights flying in a V formation across the sky. One man who is said to have flight experience who allegedly witnessed the event estimated that the lights were about a thousand feet from the ground and multiple other witnesses described the whole event as having happened in complete and total silence. The lights or whatever they were attached to made no noise at all. That makes it highly unlikely and in my opinion very improbable that airplanes or any known aircrafts that we would normally see in the sky were involved. One of the same observers, and I think it was the guy who was the pilot, called in to Luke Air Force Base about the event and was told by the operator that they had received many calls that night about the same exact event. However, according to NUFORC and their records on this partic- ular case, the base later claimed that they never received any phone calls about it. I have to wonder here, why did this one get so much attention and the last one we just talked about- that had dozens more witnesses- didn't even blip anyone's radar? Probably because the air force was notified and they felt like they needed to at least attempt to do some damage control. Again, that's just my opinion though. The Phoenix Lights received national media attention a few months later and that's when the military finally offered an explanation. They claimed that the lights were just left-over flares that the Maryland Air National Guard had dropped randomly at the end of another operation they had been conducting that night in Arizona. However, many people remain unconvinced with that explanation.

CHAPTER 22
THE TRIAL OF JOE MOODY

In 1993 a thirty-four year old real estate agent and financial planner from Tucson, Arizona named Joe Moody carried out a series of gruesome murders. In November of 93 he viciously and violently attacked and killed an acquaintance of his named Michelle Malone who was thirty three at the time. He savagely beat her and then shot her, ending her life. It was later found out that he had made her write him a check for five hundred dollars and even made her rewrite a new one when the first one had gotten her blood smeared onto it. He also stole two guns from her house. At the time he wasn't connected to the crime and most people familiar with this case feel like he more than likely would have gotten away with it if he hadn't gone on to kill again five days later. This time it was his fifty six year old neighbor, a woman named Patricia Magda. Moody slit her throat and then bludgeoned her with her own hedge clippers. Just like with his previous victim, he robbed Patricia's home. It was only after Patricia's murder that Joe Moody was arrested and put on trial for his crimes and that's when things took a turn into very bizarre territory.

People who were present in the courtroom during Joe's trial were very unsettled by him. Not only did he commit savage, brutal and horrifically nonsensical crimes, but he sat there in his chair in the courtroom the entire time with an eerie and very large grin on his face. He didn't seem like someone who was facing the death penalty for committing seemingly random murders, but more like a kid on Christmas morning as he looks under the tree and sees all of his presents for the first time. He would often wave and show off for the packed courtroom and he took himself on as a client, choosing to forego a real attorney and representing himself. Eventually Joe was questioned about his motives for committing the horrible crimes against those two seemingly random women and he claimed that he'd been visited by what he called "extrasensory biological entities," extraterrestrials,and that they'd told him to kill the women. In fact he said they did more than just tell him to do it, but that they compelled him through mind control and he really had no say in the matter at all, according to his bizarre defense. Perhaps even stranger, he wasn't trying to use this as a defense to try and get away with it or to get himself off the hook for the death penalty or at all, but he merely stated it as fact and went on to take full responsibility. He pleaded guilty to all charges against him.

Joe Moody said he welcomed the death penalty because he knew that the aliens who had compelled him to do their bidding would resurrect him with their technology, thereby finally being able to prove their existence to the human race once and for all. He went as far as to explain that the reason he'd chosen to represent himself was the fact that the attorney he'd originally had wanted him to plead not guilty by reason of insanity but he was adamant he receive the death penalty in order for the aliens to be able to bring him back to life. I have a quote from Joe Moody that reads, "We have finally come to the point where I get my birthday wish. I hope you grant the appropriate sentence to allow me to complete my mission." He showed no remorse and had no reaction when he was found guilty and sentenced to death. Unfortunately for him though the death penalty would be overturned and he would end up being sentenced to life in prison without the possibility of parole. This happened because eventually it was deemed that he'd been incompetent to represent himself at his trial and he was given a second trial with an actual attorney, where they didn't sentence him to death but to life. Joe Moody died on October 7, 2019 in prison of "unspecified causes" and most people still laugh to this day and make jokes about whether or not the extraterrestrials ever resurrected him. However, I would caution them not to just toss out the idea that they might have.

I don't know, obviously, why this man did what he did but I will never refuse to consider someone's defense simply because it sounds illogical and too far out there. I mean, look at who I am and what I do for a living. More than likely he was just insane and a sick person but there's a chance in my opinion that he was compelled to kill people, for whatever reason. As far as the extraterrestrials bringing him back from the dead is concerned, people only think about an actual body being risen but if you know anything about how things work in the paranormal community, especially when it's concerning otherworldly entities we really know nothing about, you'd know that things aren't always what they seem and a resurrection doesn't necessarily have to include the rising up of someone's physical body. What about his spirit?ov His soul or some other ethereal part of his being? All I'm saying is that, for me, it's at least in the realm of possibility that he was reunited with his extraterrestrial overlords and we really have no way of knowing one way or another.

CHAPTER 23
JOEL LANKFORD

In February of 2022 police in Georgia received a call from a panic stricken woman who was repeatedly stating that someone was trying to kill her. When they arrived on the scene they immediately noticed they were in the parking lot of a church, and the woman who called them was heavily bleeding and very terrified. Not too far away there was a vehicle with the engine running, and the wheels spinning. The doors were open but no one was inside of it. The victim herself was disoriented and she was immediately taken to the hospital while the officers searched for the perpetrators. As they were looking for the person or people who'd done that to the woman, their 911 call center received a call about a trespasser. This time the crime was happening on the front porch of a local home. The police showed up to the house just in time to apprehend a man named Joel Lankford, and it didn't take long for the authorities to figure out that this was the same man who had attacked the woman in the church parking lot whom they'd just rushed to the hospital. Joel said that aliens made him crash his car in the church lot, and that they'd transported him onto the person's porch where he had just been arrested. The officers thought immediately that something was wrong with him mentally because from the church where his vehicle had been found and where they'd found the injured and panicked woman to the porch where they'd found him was a distance of at least eighteen miles. He seemingly thought he was still there at the church and was clearly disoriented himself. His speech was slurred severely and his breath reeked like alcohol according to the official police reports, and he was eventually charged with leaving the scene of an accident, driving while intoxicated and failing to render aid. The woman eventually recovered from her wounds and ordeal and explained that she knew Joel and had been voluntarily in the car with him at the time he crashed and everything else had happened. It's still not clear why she told 911 that someone was trying to kill her and unfortunately there's nothing more to this story on the internet. This one did make me think if something strange was going on, stranger than the usual that is, because why WOULD she have claimed that someone was trying to kill her if she knew Joel and if her injuries were merely from the car accident and not actually from being attacked at all? I guess we'll never know.

CHAPTER 24
CHILDREN OF THE GRAYS

I recently came across a book called "Children of the Grays" by a man named Bret Oldman. In this book Bret details his lifelong experiences with the alien grays, as we've come to call them in modern times, and he talks about everything he'd gone through during his numerous abduction experiences. He said he can attest to the psychological, physical and emotional scars and traumas that he's had to suffer with, throughout his life, that stem from those experiences. He said that he has been having experiences with the grays specifically since he was five years old and still has abductions and other experiences happening to this very day. He also claimed to have been subjected to medical and sexual procedures and experiments even with his mind and sometimes it's all done mentally. He explains in the book the deep empathy he has for the women who deal with certain kinds of abductions by these particular extraterrestrials- the alien grays. He describes the acts done by these beings as "cold and heartless." I don't want to say that I fully disagree with him because I cannot imagine what these people and all abductees who are prone to these "experiments" go through, and most of us would refer to it as torture. With that being said, I will say from the beginning here that I'm not sure, at least from the gray's perspective, that anything they're doing is "cold and heartless." I say this because with all of the research I've done and experiences I've had with not only the grays but multiple other extraterrestrial entities throughout my life, I've come to the conclusion that these beings do not understand human emotion outside of having just a general understanding of the concept of emotions. I am certainly not excusing the behaviors or downplaying the trauma and I'm sure anguish that goes along with the abductions where they're experimenting but I just want to try and keep the separation front and center. They more than likely don't realize how cold and heartless what they're doing is and honestly probably don't even understand what those words mean. They're basically emotionless, as far as what I understand and as far as how we humans feel and deal with them.

In Bret's book there is a chapter titled "The Baby Takers" and I am going to retell an experience from it in my own words. It's a personal experience that happened to him and his girlfriend at the time and I wanna make sure you know this came from his book and the book sounds so interesting I cannot wait to read it. Bret says in the book that his girlfriend was about a week away from her fourth month of pregnancy. The pregnancy was progressing completely normally and everything was great. The baby was healthy and growing strong. Her last doctor appointment with her OBGYN had been a week before this encounter happened. He said he and his pregnant girlfriend were awoken one night in the middle of the night to a very loud bang. Our witness jumped up to see what was happening and saw four gray aliens just standing there in his bedroom. He explains that he and she were both abducted by these four extraterrestrials faster than either of them could have any sort of reaction or really before either one even knew what was going on. The next day they realized one of the aliens had knocked a typewriter down, most likely accidentally, and that's what the loud bang that initially woke them up was. Most likely the ETs didn't want them to wake up- not that it really matters with the ease with which they can completely paralyze and incapacitate us. Once abducted they were both placed in the same room and our victim was only able to move his head. He was otherwise help-less and incapacitated physically. This is where it starts to feel very evil, at least in my opinion. He claims that he was looking over at his girlfriend and immediately realized they were extracting the baby from her womb. He turned his head and claimed one of the grays took their hand and turned his head back, forcing him to watch the procedure. Bret explained, "The mental control these aliens have on you is beyond description.I could not resist their desire to have me watch the procedure. She was hysterical and begging them to stop. I was overcome with rage."

Of course the two of them then woke up in their bed the next day and his girlfriend spotted some blood on their sheets. She went to the bathroom to check and confirmed she was "bleeding some" and told Bret to call her doctor immediately. When she got to the OBGYN's office, they told her what most likely had happened was that she had lost the baby. Now, I don't want to get into specific details here because even though I am covering this in the most neutral and respectful way I possibly can, I feel like I want to keep it general, especially since I am retelling someone else's very traumatizing story here. The doctor sent them both across the street to the hospital for her to have a "clean out" and that's the best way I can put it without actually saying the words. Bret's mother went to sit with him and wait and he said that when the procedure was done and the doctor was walking down the hall towards him and his mother he looked worried or even a bit scared. His facial expression wasn't neutral as it should have been, and Bret noticed immediately that it was "off" somehow. This is a fairly common procedure for a woman to have, especially after the loss of a pregnancy, so this made our witness quite nervous and he asked the doctor if everything is okay and the doctor replied that his girlfriend was fine but that he, "had never seen anything like it" as he scratched his head and wrinkled his brow.

The doctor explained, "There was no tissue at all in the womb. It was completely clean. If I hadn't just examined her I would think that this woman had never been pregnant. I can't explain it." As the doctor turned and walked away Bret looked at his mother and said, somewhat out of the blue and surprising even himself, "They took it!" He said that though he had instant recall at that moment of everything that had occurred the night before during the abduction, he was too emotionally drained to explain it all at that time. All of this had happened in the 1980s and Bret said he found out later on in life that his girlfriend also remembered everything. They decided it was for the best for them to only tell very few, very trusted family members and friends but to otherwise keep quiet about it for fear of ridicule. This right here is how these extraterrestrials who are doing these horrible things, whether they understand it or not, are able to continue doing it for generations as far as we know and most likely for millennia or since the beginning of time as far as we know. This isn't a new phenomenon- it's ancient. Bret and his poor girlfriend were devastated and traumatized and figured no one would believe them. They hoped they'd now be left alone since the beings had, "got what they wanted." However, that wouldn't be the case for them, unfortunately.

Recently in 2012, Bret was contacted by the show Monsters and Mysteries in America. They'd asked him to come on the show and talk about the abduction experiences he had- more specifically- the event where they took the fetus from his girlfriend more than thirty years previously. He found out his now ex-girlfriend was also interviewed and the producers of the show told him she had remembered almost the exact same thing as he did even though neither had spoken of it since they were together in the eighties and neither had spoken to the other one in about as long. Bret's point in explaining this was to show that the extraterrestrials made absolutely zero attempts to try and either wipe or screen the memory of the horrible and callous things that happened that night. He firmly and fully believes the reason for this is their seemingly deep interest in and study of intense human emotions-such as the ones brought on immediately and then over time in our witness and the female victim as well. They were forcing him to watch her go through this knowing there was absolutely nothing he could do about it and then watching and studying them long term in order to possibly better understand their concept of humanity and our vast range of emotions. Honestly though, no one knows why they do what they do and that's just my best educated guess. Bret agreed to do the show and when the segment aired more people than ever before were privy to his private ordeal, but I don't think he cared at that point.

Bret's book was published not too long after his segment on the show aired. He explains that the cover of his book depicts a small, hybrid female whom the grays had introduced him to. It didn't take long for people all over the world to start contacting him and relating to his experiences, particularly the one from that fateful night when they forced him to watch them take what he thought was his baby out of his girlfriend's body. I assume he loved her deeply and this had to have torn him apart. The people contacting Bret about all of this were from all walks of life and many of them were your average, normal human beings working regular jobs. Nothing seemingly unique or extraordinary about them. Not on the surface anyway as all of them had been keeping these horrible experiences to themselves for fear of ridicule. I mean they were flight attendants, doctors, teachers and lawyers and they would possibly risk unemployment and losing everything they've worked for their whole lives had they mentioned what had happened to them. It's disgusting and makes me so angry but I do believe wholeheartedly that the alien involved realize that most human beings will do this and therefore they are able to leave the memories, in extreme detail, completely intact in order to continue on with not only their stealing of fetuses but their work in trying to comprehend and study our intense and very wide range of emotions. That's my opinion but it's not an uncommon or unpopular one. Bret stated about the people contacting him,

"These people were police, flight attendants, teachers, lawyers and so on. They were regular everyday people who could be your neighbor. You would never know that these horrible things had been done to them. Just like I did for so many years, they were keeping quiet. Most of them hadn't even told immediate family members. They had no one to turn to for help. All of them lived in fear of ridicule. They feared they would lose their jobs or be diagnosed with some severe mental illness and placed under care and supervision in a mental health care facility."

Bret then goes on to include some of the cases and experiences of the people he was communicating with. He tells of one woman who got in touch with him who said she had become mysteriously pregnant when she was just a teenager. Her parents were furious and of course they didn't believe her when she was just as shocked and confused as they were and insisted she had never even had sex before. This woman explained that she too had had her fetus taken from her at approximately twelve weeks and that she too was awake and alert during the entire experience and she was also made to remember the entire, harrowing and traumatizing ordeal. The very next day she told her parents what had happened with having been abducted and the fetus being stolen from her womb by the extraterrestrials. They had her committed to a mental institution. Ladies and gentlemen this right here is still the unfortunate and devastating reality in which we live. Many of the people who came forward and contacted Bret with their encounter stories were all reporting almost the exact same thing. Some of them even claimed they were abducted again and made to spend time with or were at the very least introduced to hybrid children that either looked just like them or closely resembled somehow the hybrid child on the cover of his book. Were they all made to meet this "child" and if so, what role did she play? Some women even claimed to have had more than one and even, in some cases, several, fetuses taken from them throughout their lives. Most of them say that they've been abducted ever since in order to spend time with the stolen baby/child.

There's another element to all of this too guys and Bret said that so many people, himself included, who have had multiple abduction experiences throughout their lives, also report forced sexual encounters with hybrids. Many of the women claimed to have been sexually assaulted, then becoming pregnant from it and then, eventually around twelve weeks pregnant, having the fetus forcibly and surgically removed during yet another abduction experience. See, here is where it gets a bit complicated because most of the time when we hear about abduction encounters, when it comes to the hybrids and seeding programs at least, we hear about the painful and almost torturous removal of sperm or eggs from the human subject and a lot of the time in those cases the person will only remember after some time has passed and not right away. Those memories, in some or maybe even in most cases, are wiped or screened.

Bret explained that the sexual attacks and experiments happen more often than the general public believes or knows about. He goes on to say that it is much more than hybrid and seeding too, saying, "The concept and study of human sexuality and emotions play heavy into the equation of the Greys interest in us." He finishes the article with, "The aliens we call the Greys are creating an alien/human hybrid species. The Greys are interested in the human body as a physical specimen. They are interested in human sexuality and our emotional makeup. Obviously, I've witnessed and experienced much more than I can relate in this short article. Countless others all over the planet have too, but are too afraid to come out publicly with their stories. Alien abductions are real, as is their hybridization program. The full implications of both remain to be seen."

CHAPTER 25
MINNIE

A Scottish woman we will be calling "Minnie" for the sake of her privacy and with respect for her anonymity, lives in a town located almost remarkably close to Loch Ness, which depending on how you look at it that could be another dot that may need connecting but for now let's just focus on the her strange encounter. It was 2007 when she claims to have had her encounter and she said it was a warm and clear summer day. She was walking her dog along the hills that overlook Loch Ness itself when something truly bizarre happened. From the description she gave of what she saw, it seems as though she was staring right at what we have all come to know as a gray alien. She first saw it from a distance of a couple of hundred feet away and thought at first glance that it was a small child. She mainly came to this conclusion because of how short it was. She walked closer to it despite her dog refusing to move even an inch closer to whatever this thing was. It was then that she realized she was not staring at a child, or at least not a human one and she froze with fear and dread just as her dog had done a few steps behind her. Minnie made eye contact with the being and they stood there for quite a while, locked in a sort of staring contest or something, when the entity suddenly reached its arms out to her.

The second the gray alien's arms were fully outstretched, Minnie stated that she watched as it transformed, almost instantaneously, into a large gray owl. It was "impossibly large;" the size of a full grown man. It all happened so fast and as soon as the transformation from strange alien to supersized owl was complete, the alien/bird thing took off faster than humanly possible into the skies and flew right over Loch Ness. As Minnie watched on in fear and a sense of awe and wonder all mixed together, it disappeared from sight into the trees and possibly altogether. She hadn't been able to see where, exactly, it had gone and couldn't even wager a guess except to say that it disappeared into the sky at a rapid speed. That wouldn't be the end of it though and Minnie's account is about to get a lot more interesting.

Minnie is one hundred percent sure that she did not experience any missing time at all and that her memories of the event are true and accurate and in perfect order, again with nothing missing. Before I go any further I'll posit this though- do we know or would we know if there was missing time? Minnie is completely sure that she has no vague or foggy memories of a strange craft or any other beings or entities, no hazy experiments being performed on her- reproductive or otherwise. No bad dreams or nightmares involving any of this either and she is adamant her memory is correct, complete and one hundred percent accurate and intact. A small, short gray alien being outstretching its arms, turning into a gigantic owl and flying away, across the loch and disappearing into the woods is what she'd repeatedly claimed to have witnessed that day, time and time again. Minnie has since come up with a very interesting theory as to what happened to her and I'm interested to know what everyone else will make of this one. Many people who have listened to her story and to what she believes happened to her that day so long ago think that she's trying extremely hard to give regular or ordinary meaning to her surreal and extraordinary encounter that day, but I'll let you all be the judge.

She believes and again I tend to agree, that extraterrestrials, or at the very least the grays, have the ability to shapeshift into anything they want to become at any given time. She believes she just happened to see an owl and that in this owl, or whatever other form, they are able to very easily spy on humanity and specifically abductees and hybrids as well. Believe it or not the list is very long of the forms, mainly animals, that extraterrestrials in general are supposedly able to take on. It's mainly cats though-black cats especially! However there's also owls, german shepherd dogs and even deer. That's just a few of the many but that's what Minnie believes. Maybe this entity was there to spy on her or someone else who was in the area that day and she just happened to have been the one to spot it. If this is true, or even if it's to be believed at all, how would we ever know without the eye witness testimonies of people like Minnie who witness it with their very own eyes?

CHAPTER 26
BETTY AND BARNEY
HILL (PART ONE)

The 1961 abduction of Betty and Barney Hill is possibly one of the most well known abductions in our history and some say it's the one that really set things off for the field of ufology- with professional and normal, average, everyday people coming forward and unabashedly speaking publicly about the things happening to and around them. It basically is to abductions what Roswell is to crashed ufos. My initial reason for looking into the case was because I came across some information that says the Hill case might've actually been them just being more victims of MK Ultra experiments but when I went back to look at that information all of the articles I had saved were suddenly missing or they came up as nonexistent and I didn't know where to go with it. I'm going to continue looking into that and researching some more but I thought for now we could talk about the abduction itself and what happened to this poor couple. It's undeniable that something happened to them that night so long ago and their story is still one that's discussed and debated throughout the field of ufology and beyond,

On September 19th, 1961 a couple from New Hampshire named Betty and Barney Hill were driving back to their home, along with their dog Delsey, after vacationing in Montreal, Canada. Betty was a social worker and Barney worked for the USPS and while they were making their way home, at around 10:30 pm and as they drove south of Lancaster, NH, they were surprised to see a very strange sight in the sky above them and ahead just a little bit. At first Betty thought it was nothing more than a fallen or shooting star but then realized it was shooting up into the sky and not falling down from it. It puzzled them and they looked through their binoculars to try and get a better idea at what they were looking at. The lighted object wasn't any sort of familiar aircraft- commercial or military- and looked wholly and completely different from anything they had ever seen or encountered before. They continued driving through the mountains but as they did they both became overwhelmed with fear and by the idea that whoever was piloting the strange craft was playing some sort of game with them and watching them as they went along the route towards home. They felt like the flying disc shaped craft was almost goading them to follow along with its maneuvers.

Betty urged Barney to stop the car so that they could get out and get a better look and also so they could walk their dog. He pulled over at a small picnic area and scenic lookout, just south of Twin Mountain. They had pulled over already and were completely vulnerable and exposed in the middle of the road on a dark mountain pass. It was a very dangerous situation even without the strange flying disc and I can't imagine the terror of these two people as this situation unfolded right in front of them. Betty looked through the binoculars and saw an "odd shaped" craft with flashing multicolored lights flying over the face of the moon. Barney would later describe the craft as being "pancake-looking" and he and his wife both agreed it also looked like something from out of this world- "unearthly" is what they called it. Barney had already pulled the binoculars out again and was closely watching the ship through them as it hovered in the sky and continued to approach them. They got back into the car and drove away, continuing to head home and hoping to outrun the strange aerial vehicle. They prayed that once they moved past it, they would never have to see the strange craft again. The Hills drove through the very quiet and isolated area of Franconia Notch but when they noticed the craft up above them in the sky again, they started driving very slowly in order to keep an eye on and get a good look at it. They watched in awe and silence as the silent and illuminated craft bounced back and forth in the sky up above them and they realized too at that point that it was rotating. About one mile south of Indian Head the object suddenly rapidly descended towards their vehicle and once it stopped, hovering about ninety feet above them in mid air- silently- the craft took up everything inside the view of the giant windshield of their 1957 Chevy BelAir.

Barney had his pistol on him and exited the vehicle, approaching it to get a better look through the binoculars at what they were dealing with. As he focused on the craft through the lenses of the binoculars, he counted at least eight to as many as eleven humanoid beings. All of them were wearing little black caps and glossy black uniforms as they milled around and stared directly at him and his wife through the windows of the craft. In unison, all but one of the figures moved to what looked like a panel on the rear wall of the hallway that encircled the front portion of the craft. The one figure that didn't move continued staring at Barney through the lenses of the binoculars and telepathically communi-cated a message to him, "stay where you are, and keep looking." The voice was calm and even toned- even a little reassuring. Red lights on what appeared to be bat-winged fins came out of the sides of the crafts like two telescopes, and a long structure that looked somewhat like a walking plank or something similar, descended out of the bottom of the craft itself as well. The silent craft once again started approaching the vehicle and Barney himself and he estimated that it came within about fifty to eighty feet overhead of them and approximately three hundred feet away from them. Barney yelled to his wife that the "things" inside the machine were planning to kidnap them. The pair, who had gotten out of the car to get a better look, jumped quickly back into it and sped off at a very high and dangerous rate of speed. They had no idea if they would be able to outrun the craft in the sky but knew they needed to at least try. After all, making an effort was better than just standing there and allowing themselves to be taken. At first it seemed like they had made the right decision because it appeared as though neither the craft nor the crew within it had followed them.

I'm not sure if the couple breathed sighs of relief or not but I hope they didn't because this traumatic ordeal was only just beginning. It didn't take long after they sped away for them to realize that something was very wrong with their journey. They arrived home just before dawn and they had some odd sensations and things going on with them that they couldn't explain or understand. Betty insisted that their luggage had to be kept by the back door rather than in the main part of the house. If that's being brought up as her exhibiting odd behavior then I guess that was uncommon for her to do. The watches they wore that night would never work again and Barney said he noticed that the leather strap to his binoculars was torn, even though he had no memory of how it had gotten that way. He had been wearing his best dress shoes and the toes of them were all scuffed and scraped. They had been shining and like brand new when they left their vacation and got in the car to drive home and he had no memory of it happening or even how it could have. Both Barney and Betty said they felt a strange compulsion to go into the bathroom and examine his genitals, though they found nothing unusual when they did so. They definitely thought something sinister had happened to them but they had no memory of it. They both took very long showers to try and remove any sort of radiation contamination they thought they could have possibly been exposed to and they each drew a picture of what they remembered observing, as far as the craft they had seen was concerned.

They were absolutely perplexed and tried time and again to go over the chronology of events from when they first saw the craft in the sky until they got home but couldn't do it. When they tried to remember anything from that night- from the missing time- they would immediately start to hear a strange buzzing sound and their memories remained fragmented and incomplete. They went to sleep for a few hours and as soon as she woke up, Betty took the clothing she had been wearing for the drive home back out from where she'd hung it in her closet. She then saw that her dress had been torn at the zipper, hem and lining and later on when she took the dress out again to look at it, she noticed there was some sort of pink powdery substance on the dress itself which she wasn't able to identify. She hung the dress on a clothes-line and the pink powder blew away but the dress was damaged beyond repair. She would never be able to wear it again. At first she threw it away but immediately thought better of it, retrieving it from the trash and hanging it back in her closet. Throughout the years five different laboratories conducted chemical analysis on that dress but nothing was ever found. As for the vehicle, there were shiny concentric circles on the trunk that they knew for certain hadn't been there just the day before all of it had happened and for whatever reason, they got it in their mind to take a compass outside and put it near the circles on the car. Whenever it would get near them, the needle would whirl rapidly. However, when they moved even just a few inches away from the shiny spots, the compass would go back to acting normal again. According to one source I read, "Walter N. Webb, a Boston astronomer and NICAP member, met with the Hills on October 21, 1961. In a six-hour interview, the Hills related all they could remember of the UFO encounter. Barney stated that he had developed a "mental block", and that he suspected there were some portions of the event that he did not wish to remember. He described in detail all that he could remember about the craft and the appearance of the "somehow not human" figures aboard it. Webb stated that "they were telling the truth and the incident probably occurred exactly as reported except for some minor uncertainties and technicalities that must be tolerated in any such observations where human judgment is involved (e.g., exact time and length of visibility, apparent sizes of object and occupants, distance and height of object, etc.)."

CHAPTER 27
BETTY AND BARNEY HILL (PART TWO)

Ten days after the UFO encounter, Betty began having a series of very vivid dreams and those dreams continued for five successive nights. She said she experienced the dreams with such detail and intensity like she had never experienced dreams before. On the fifth night the dreams stopped for good but even though she never dreamt of any of it again, both the dreams and the event, along with the missing time, occupied her thoughts constantly and consistently throughout each day. When she would mention the dreams to Barney he was sympathetic but not at all concerned and eventually she just stopped talking about it. In November of that year, Betty- still obsessively thinking about those dreams- started to write down the details of them and one part of the dream specifically stood out to her. In it, the Hills encountered a road block just up ahead of where the craft had approached them- when Barney yelled to her that they were about to be kidnapped, and at the roadblock there were men that surrounded their car. She lost consciousness but struggled and fought to regain it and did. When she came to again she was being forced by two small men to walk into the forest at night and she saw Barney behind her. She called out to him but he didn't respond and she said he had either been sleepwalking or in a trance. The men who were marching them through the woods were described by Betty as five foot to five foot four inches tall and they all wore matching blue uniforms and matching caps- just like the ones military cadets were known to wear at the time. They appeared to be almost human, with black hair, dark eyes, prominent noses and lips that had a bluish tint to them. However, their skin was gray. The next thing she knew she and Barney were being taken back to their car, where one of the men suggested to them that they wait for the craft to depart before they themselves left the area. They did as they were told and once they could no longer see the strange craft in the sky they drove home.

Here's where the missing time comes into play. Investigators who had read Webb's initial report had a few questions for the Hills. Now, I am not completely familiar with this case and the names of these investigators were Jackson and Hohman but I couldn't find who they were with. I believe it could have been the local police or it could have been the military but either way, they had questions about the length of the trip that night. The Hills had already noted that they had arrived home some time later than they had anticipated, but they hadn't initially realized they had arrived home an entire three hours later. The drive was one hundred and seventy eight miles and should have reasonably taken them about four hours. It was only with these questions being asked of them that they realized that it had taken them seven hours to get home from the time they left Colebrook until they got to their house. They had stopped a couple of times, as we've already discussed but it wasn't for any serious length of time that they weren't driving. When Hohman and Jackson noted that discrepancy to the Hills they had no explanation for it. This is the perfect example of what we are talking about in this community when we use the words "missing time." The Hills remembered nothing about the thirty five miles they spent traversing US Route 3 between Lincoln/Indian Head and Ashland. Both of them did say they remembered an image of a fiery orb sitting on the ground. Both of them reasoned that it must have been the moon but, this doesn't make sense for obvious reasons. I wonder if that was an implanted thought. Like "oh don't worry, that's just the moon. It's fine!" Either way the investigators informed them that the moon had already set by then, much earlier in the night, but the Hills still had no explanation for the two men about any of it. The subject of hypnosis was brought up and everyone agreed that it would be helpful for them to undergo hypnotic regression so that they could recover previously irretrievable memories. Barney kind of didn't want to do it at all and was apprehensive about it. However, he eventually agreed to go along with it, thinking it might help Betty with what he called, "that nonsense with her dreams."

On November 23, 1962 the Hills attended a meeting at the parsonage of their church, where Captain Ben H Swett was the guest speaker. Swett was from the United States Air Force and it had come up in his speech that he was interested in hypnotism and regressions and that he himself was a board certified hypnotist. After he spoke the Hills approached him and told them everything that had happened to them up to that point; their whole strange story. The captain seemed to be particularly interested in the part of their ordeal that involved the missing time. The Hills asked him if he would be interested in hypnotizing them but he declined. He cautioned them not to go to an amateur hypnotist for such an important undertaking and admitted that's exactly what he was. He only didn't do it because he thought they needed someone much more experienced than he was and I respect him for that and for at least being honest about his capabilities, realizing how important it was that those two get the best help available to them at the time for such a serious undertaking and important event.

In January of 1964 the Hills would go and see Dr. Benjamin Simon from Boston, Massachusetts and he would be the one to recover the repressed memories once and for all. Let's talk first about Barney's sessions. His hypnosis was consistent with his conscious recall. He reported that his binocular strap had been broken when he ran back to the car after realizing the beings were planning on abducting him and his wife. He recalled driving away- speeding off- to get away from the UFO but then feeling an overwhelming urge to pull over to the side of the road a little while afterwards. Once he gave in to the irresistible compulsion, he saw five men standing there on the side of the road right where he had pulled over. He hadn't turned the car off yet but it stalled as soon as he saw the men and that's when three of the men approached the vehicle. He described them similarly to how Betty had, and during the first hypnosis session he said that they stared into his eyes with a terrifying and mesmerizing effect. He said, "Oh those eyes! They're there in my brain!" One of the other things he said during that first session was, "I was told to close my eyes because I saw two eyes coming close to mine, and I felt like the eyes had pushed into my eyes." During his second hypnosis session Barney said, "All I see are these eyes…. I'm not even afraid that they're not even connected to a body. They're just there. They're just up close to me, pressing up against my eyes." While Betty reported conversation with the leader of the group of creatures in English, Barney said he heard them speaking in some sort of gibberish. A mumbling language he couldn't understand. Betty also mentioned the same thing when Barney said he had communicated with them in English. The few times they did communicate with him, it was mostly through "thought transference." He was unfamiliar with the word telepathy at the time.

Under hypnosis, Betty's accounts were very similar to all of the aforementioned dreams she'd had. There were a couple of notable differences though, mainly relating to her capture and release. Also, the technology on the craft was described differently during her hypnosis sessions, the sequential order of the abduction differed and the appearance of the men was drastically different from anything in her dreams or that she had previously reported. I wonder if this is just because the dreams were maybe only some- what breaking through whatever shield or screen the aliens had implanted in her and Barney to keep them from remembering. Like, maybe they thought okay, let's put this information in her mind in case she starts having dream recall, or something like that. For the most part and overall, both Barney and Betty's hypnosis memories lined up with one another's and were very consistent. The Hills basically went back to living regular lives and though they would talk about their experience with people they knew, they were reluctant to speak publicly about it. There's more information on the Hills experience but for the most part this is the jist of it all.

I'd like to ask you all a question. If you were to close your eyes and imagine an alien abduction in your heads right now, what would it look like? For the most part, and of course there are exceptions, this question might conjure up thoughts about a person out in the middle of nowhere, probably alone, who suddenly sees something strange in the sky and is then beamed up into a giant beam of light. Maybe the images of someone waking in the night to see a strange being inside of their bedroom only to then be beamed somehow through the walls or ceiling of the home and into a spaceship waiting silently outside? Many of the strangest abductions happen outdoors but not necessarily under the circumstances one might normally think of. All I'm saying is, basically, nowhere is safe and neither is anyone. These types of things have been known to happen all over the world, at all hours of the day and night and to all different kinds of people. There's no one formula for it, and for me that's what makes it so much more terrifying. Before we move on I would like to point anyone interested in knowing more about this particular case to YouTube, where if you search for it you can find the audio recordings of Betty and Barney's hypnotic regression sessions.

CHAPTER 28
THE DERBYSHIRE BBQ

One summer evening in 1995 a group of friends was barbecuing in the backyard of a suburban home in Derbyshire, in the east midlands of England. They'd been having a great time and just hanging out with one another until around 10:30pm, when things took a turn for the highly strange. The witnesses later said that a very large, disc shaped craft had descended from the sky, stopping to hover over their party. After that happened, all of them felt extremely sick all of the sudden, with nausea and uncontrollable vomiting. They said there was some missing time involved as well, and one of the witnesses noticed that the grill or the barbecue itself had been burning brightly one moment and the very next it was cold and nothing but ash. There had been food cooking on it and it was cold and burned to a crisp too. They all noticed the food on the grill and when they looked at their watches they realized they had lost an hour and a half of time and none of them could remember what had happened during it or where it had gone. In the following days, all of them would also be plagued by horrible nightmares that terrified them and they all struggled with feelings of crippling anxiety that they couldn't escape from. I don't know who initially suggested that maybe they be hypnotized but they all agreed nonetheless and they were anxious to finally find out what had happened to them in those ninety minutes they couldn't remember. They were all regressed separately and yet they remembered the same things for the most part. They had been brought aboard a strange craft where they were subjected to terrible examinations in rooms that looked like some sort of old fashioned operating theater but with walls that were "round but divided into squares." A few of the people even remembered being brought to other planets but I don't have more detailed information on that, unfortunately. Kind of makes you wonder what really happened and what became of those people.

CHAPTER 29
HELEN THOMAS AND HER MOTHER CAROL

I always wonder how abductees are chosen or why they're chosen. It's hard for me to believe that it's completely and totally random but a lot of the time it seemingly is just that simple. Here's a very strange account of someone being abducted from a residential, urban area. In March of 1988 there was a woman named Helen Thomas who came forward and said she and her mother, Carol were out near Birmingham, England and they were heading to work together. The two women took a little shortcut through a residential alleyway as they made their way to their respective jobs at a nearby mill. They walked through that alleyway a lot but that day they suddenly started to hear a strange and very loud humming sound that reverberated all around them and all at once a blinding light shot down on them from somewhere from above. The women were suddenly extremely nauseous and dizzy and as soon as they both started feeling that they just couldn't bear it anymore, the light disappeared just as suddenly as it had appeared in the first place. The sounds were gone right along with it too. The two women's relief didn't last very long because they soon realized something strange had happened to them but they couldn't remember any of it. They noticed that several hours had passed and Helen's jacket was wet even though they hadn't been or gone anywhere near water- as far as they knew anyway. It hadn't rained and they weren't even near anything wet. Over the next few days both women experienced strange and painful blisters all over their bodies and welts too that seemingly appeared out of nowhere and for no known reason. They suffered nosebleeds and a strange discharge leaked from their belly buttons. They eventually talked about what had happened to them to a UFO researcher named Tony Todd and he was convinced that they had been abducted.

Tony arranged for the women to be hypnotically regressed and under hypnosis things would only become more bizarre. They were finally able to remember what happened to them during all those missing hours that day. The women said that after the light beam shot down on them, it engulfed them and they were suddenly inside of a bright, white room where they were lying naked on tables next to one another, covered only in "wet netted cloths." All around them were strange looking beings with large heads, long and thin arms and wrinkled, wet skin. There was a different looking being in the corner of the room and it almost looked human. It had blonde hair, blue eyes and was wearing what looked like some sort of silver uniform with some type of insignia on it that they couldn't quite make out. (This is the typical image of what we've come to know as the Nordic aliens in our modern day.) The creatures were pushing glass tubes into the women's belly buttons and even though the women didn't know what it all meant, they both separately said that they thought that the beings were "taking eggs" from them. One of the creatures then examined Helen's leather jacket and was seemingly fascinated with it. It began rubbing it all over its body. When the examination and alleged egg harvesting were finished, the women were shown some sort of display that was covered in strange symbols and that showed horrible images of war and violence. They were then dropped off right back in the alleyway they had originally been taken from. I don't even know what to say to that. It always confuses me when people remember being shown either images from the past or the alleged future, wars and death and all that- when they're shown anything at all- but yet are made to instantly forget it the moment they are dropped off back on earth. What's the point of that I wonder? I mean, they show it to people all the time, all sorts of things, and then don't allow the people to remember any of it anyway. Seems counter-productive but then again, I don't pretend to understand much of what happens in these scenarios.

CHAPTER 30
TRAVIS WALTON (PART ONE)

The Travis Walton case is considered by most people to be the first really verifiable alien abduction and it was the inspiration for the Blockbuster movie called "Fire in the Sky." I had to break this one down into several parts because of how long it is. Travis Walton was from Snowflake, Arizona and was around twenty two years old when this alleged abduction took place. In and around his hometown in Snowflake he gained himself quite the reputation of kind of a "bad boy". He would ride his motorcycle too fast through and around town, he was an amateur boxer and a wild bull rider. These were just some of his unorthodox, especially for the time, pastimes. Just to give you an idea of how "wild" Travis' reputation was I'll tell you about one time when Travis and his friends were driving down a backroad at night and a bear ran out of the woods and into the middle of the road and stopped directly in front of the vehicle Travis and some of his friends were in. According to all who were present, Travis without hesitation upon seeing this gigantic bear randomly landed in the middle of the road in front of the car, so it was essentially blocking their way from continuing further on, jumped out of the car and gave chase to this massive wild bear. But Travis wasn't content to just scare the bear out of the roadway so he and his friends could continue on driving down it, oh no! Travis actually continued to chase this bear once it had run into the woods already. So, this is just one of many stories recounted about Travis and how he gained that bad boy rep back in those days, the days before he became possibly the most famous UFO abductee in the world. It wasn't the best or most credible reputation is what I'm getting at here and I just want you to keep that in the back of your mind as we go forward with this case/encounter. When it came to his friends however, Travis was definitely loved and respected and they all thought he was just a fun loving guy who liked adventure and acting a bit crazy from time to time. I mean, think about it, even now, what twenty two year old young man doesn't get up to some trouble or shenanigans every once in a while, especially when a group of other young men in the same age group are around? He was known as a genuinely good guy, don't get me wrong, just maybe had a bit of a troubled reputation in town due to his wild and crazy activities and loud motorcycle.

In 1975 Travis worked as a logger. Basically he and about six of his coworkers/friends would get contracted to go out into the wilderness and clear trees. They were a very small and basic operation though and actually used axes and chainsaws for most of the jobs they did. They weren't some super huge company with expensive and fancy equipment. Think about this too; how physically fit and strong one would have to be to be able to do this kind of work on a regular basis, as a full time job. With this being such a strenuous and even dangerous job, the crew boss named Mike Rogers, spoke about the incident with Travis and was very clear that he and the six other men who were a part of this crew, including Travis himself, had to be absolutely clear and level headed in order to efficiently and effectively do their job. Not to mention to be able to do the job responsibly and safely as well. Mike stated that he knew these other guys he worked with were mentally sound and stable bc he hired them, and he knew they were bc they had to be, otherwise they never would've been working with him that day or any other. Mental health was actually a big component in obtaining these positions and it was something Mike took very seriously and paid very close attention to. Basically if he felt something wasn't quite right, so to speak, he wouldn't hire someone on because the physical strain could easily cause a not so balanced person to absolutely lose it and/or possibly endanger himself or one of the other workers on the crew with him. So Mike was vouching for the other witnesses and Travis himself when it comes to the men's mental state and frame of mind not only on the date but up until the abduction allegedly took place.

On November 5, 1975 Mike Rogers was given a contract to clear out twelve hundred acres of land inside the Apache-Sitgreaves National Forest right there near Snowflake, Arizona. Mike said from the very beginning he told all of the men in his small crew that this job was a massive undertaking for their little company and to expect to be working long hours and doing some pretty strenuous work. After all, they did have a schedule to keep. Just to give you an idea of how basic these men had to work, their one and only company vehicle was a regular sized pickup truck that held all seven men and their equipment. So, despite working these very long hours without almost any breaks at all, by the third day the men were behind schedule. At the end of the third day, the men, who had just worked a pretty much non-stop shift the past few days at a breakneck and grueling pace were just beyond exhausted by the end of it. All seven of them helped clean everything up and after they'd finished and loaded the tools up into the back of the truck, the seven of them climbed aboard and drove to the access road they took to get into the clearing area in the first place. Remember these are deep woods, and this was an area deep into the forest they were clearing out. Before they made it to the main road however, the men saw what appeared to be a bunch of random lights just hovering in the middle of the forest off to their right side. Later on the men would recount how, although they definitely all noticed these lights, it didn't strike any of them as necessarily something sinister or unusual at first. It basically didn't register to them that something was seriously wrong for a little while. They continued driving down the access road but for whatever reason, it's still unclear, they simply felt as though they couldn't ignore the strange lights anymore and wanted to get a closer look and figure out what they were. They can't say for sure if it got bigger or brighter or if it seemed as though it was sort of following them etc. For whatever reason though, they all suddenly couldn't take their eyes off of it. One of the men even commented that it must be a full moon. Another man turned and looked out the left window, so on the left side of the truck and he saw the moon over on that side of the truck and told the others that there was no way what they were looking at was the moon because the moon was on the left side and couldn't also be fully formed the way it was right ahead of them as well. The men kept trying to figure out and guess what the light was, and it seems like it had their full curiosity and attention. They already ruled out the moon. They also decided that it couldn't have been a forest fire because of the absence of smoke. So, Travis (who remember once jumped out of a vehicle and chased a massive bear back into the woods) said that they should just drive in that direction right up to whatever it was and check it out. Now, by that time the men really wanted to know what the giant light was that was seemingly coming from the absolute middle of nowhere in this giant and dense forest. After just a minute or two of hesitation on the other men's parts, they finally agreed to take the road they knew led to that section of forest and go and see what this thing was. Keep in mind too, none of them were even beginning to think or imagine that the light was something bad or ominous in any way. It literally could've been anything at this point, but not a single one of them felt or thought that they were in any kind of danger. The men were exhausted and possibly didn't have all of their wits about them at that time. It's possible they wouldn't have made the same decision had they been well rested, but that's just speculation on my part.

They turned onto the other access road which took them directly to the clearing where these lights were. Later when each man was given a polygraph test, separately I might add, when asked what it was they saw when they entered this clearing, they all described almost exactly the same thing. Human minds all remember things differently and even in the retelling of the most specific things, everyone will remember some things slightly differently than another person who is also telling the truth and saw the exact same thing. The men described seeing a disc shaped craft with large light panels in a semi circle shape underneath. The object or "craft" was just hovering there, in the clearing, up in the air perfectly still and completely silent. It was estimated to be hovering anywhere from fifty to one hundred feet off of the ground. When interviewed later on the men would describe what struck them the most was how it was like the object was suspended, frozen in the air and completely defying gravity. They were more taken aback by that fact than anything else, including the fact that this random disc shaped craft was even there in the first place. One of the men happened to be really good with structural engineering and had even built houses on the side. Not an architect but more like in construction, and he would comment at length about the incredible structure of the thing and the amazing craftsmanship and engineering that it seemed to have and be made with. The men were literally awestruck at the beauty of it. Travis, being Travis, the "adrenaline junkie" that he was, was REALLY stoked and excited about what they were seeing in front of them. It's not even that any of them knew what they were really looking at, they basically had no idea, but they instinctively knew that it was something big. Before the truck could even come to a full stop, Travis opened his door and jumped out. He unhesitatingly started taking several steps towards the craft. The other six men chose at that point to remain in the vehicle. This "craft" was about seventy five feet away from them and as I stated earlier about fifty to one hundred feet above their heads. It was totally and completely stationary at that point too, as Travis began to walk towards it. All of the men were completely silent and aside from Travis who appeared absolutely awestruck by whatever this thing was that he was walking towards. The vehicle was at a complete stop and parked by this point now as well.

Travis would later state in an interview, when asked what motivated him to start walking towards this unidentified craft, that he was definitely frightened but his curiosity had gotten the better of him. He stated that he knew instinctively that whatever they were encountering here, whatever this was, was something uncommon, not normal if you will, and that it was something unknown and spectacular. He was really curious and said he simply felt like he needed to get a better look. He was trying to make sense of what this thing was, of what his eyes were seeing because his brain couldn't identify what it was. Travis continued nonstop to take steps towards the hovering light. At some point the rest of the men came out of their initial daze and realized what Travis was doing, that he was actually approaching this thing, and they sprung into action all at once to try and stop him. All six of them said that they had instantly gotten an overwhelming feeling that something bad was going to happen and they all started yelling simultaneously for Travis to turn around and get back into the truck. Obviously, having never encountered anything like this before, they couldn't be sure, but they just had a feeling that being inside the truck was most likely safer than walking towards the thing and approaching it. After all, they didn't know who or what, if anything, was occupying this unidentified flying object. In their defense, it was floating in the air, it's quite reasonable to believe something or someone was operating or flying it, right? The men who remained in the truck stated their main concern at that point actually was, "what if this thing falls on him?" So, they were all yelling for him to come back and get into the truck and to stop approaching this weird object hovering above them in the sky. However, Travis wasn't listening and continued to approach it. Travis said that while he heard them shouting for him to come back, it's almost like he was so incredibly struck by the beauty of this machine, with all of the light panels and just as I said before the craftsmanship was like nothing any of them, including Travis had ever seen before, and it was almost like he physically couldn't pull himself away from it. From what I know from my research, Travis might have been compelled to keep walking towards the craft by whatever was inside of it and piloting it.

Eventually Travis was directly underneath the craft and he looked up when all of the sudden it started spinning rapidly around and around right on top of him as he stared straight up at it, still in awe and wonder of it. As the thing started spinning, it also started making an extremely loud noise which the men later described as " sounding mechanical." At this point, the men left in the truck were in a complete panic about Travis being directly under and so close to it and so they started screaming and shouting at the top of their lungs for him to turn back. This is when Travis said that he "kind of snapped out of it" and realized that he definitely needed to turn around and quickly get back to the truck with his friends. Just as Travis went to turn to start walking back to the truck, the bottom of the craft opened up and a beam of light shot out of it and landed directly on Travis. It was described almost like a lightning strike because it literally blew Travis about twenty feet away from it. Keep in mind that everything I've covered so far was included in the polygraph tests each man would later receive and each one was said, according to the polygraphs, to be telling the truth about all of it. Mike was in the driver seat at that time and he panicked and decided to just take off and leave Travis there. He later said he almost wasn't thinking about it and was just trying to get out of there and away from whatever the thing in the sky was. Mike slammed his foot on the gas and floored it out of there. As they were fleeing the scene, they were all trying to convince themselves that there is no possible way Travis could've survived what had just happened to him, whatever it was that had actually happened, because they didn't even really know at that point. They were all trying to convince themselves and each other that Travis had to have been dead and that there was no point in putting themselves at risk by turning and going back for him. They decided to go and get help and then come back to find

Travis' remains. These grown, super strong, kinda burly men who literally cut down trees with axes were hysterically crying at that point. They were scared, and they honestly thought that Travis was dead. Eventually though, before they could even get to the main road, Mike said he came to his senses and slammed on the brakes. He announced that he was going back for Travis. Whether Travis was dead at that point or not, he was thinking about if he needed help. What if he was only seriously injured and waiting for them to go and come back with help would be the difference between life and death for him? That is what Mike said was running through his mind as he sat there and told the others his plan to go back to the light and find their friend. He offered to let the other five men out of the truck right where he stopped and gave them an out. He said he wouldn't force them to return for Travis with him but that he was going either way. He explained if they didn't wanna go back with him that was fine and he understood but he couldn't in good conscience just leave Travis there not knowing if he's dead or alive and or if he possibly needs medical attention. All of the men decided that standing out in the open in the middle of a dark forest was definitely not a better idea than at least being all together in the relative safety (they assumed) of the truck and they all agreed to turn back and look for Travis.

Once they got back to the spot however, there wasn't a UFO anywhere to be seen anymore. They get out of the truck and despite looking everywhere for Travis they couldn't find him anywhere. They were all presumably in complete state shock and disbelief at that point at what they had just been witness to. Mike was still uncontrollably crying because he felt so incredibly guilty they'd just left Travis behind the way they did. The men were now in a panic about what had become of Travis because despite running around the forest looking for either Travis or any sign of him and screaming his name at the top of their lungs over and over again, they couldn't find any trace of him. There seemed to be no evidence at all of what they'd just witnessed there only a few short minutes ago. After looking for a little while they all decided they had to go directly to the authorities and tell them what had happened. They knew they needed help with help trying to find Travis, or what they felt was gonna be his remains at that point. Don't think for a second they didn't realize how bad this was gonna look for them when they went to the police and reported Travis as missing and told this story as to what had happened, but they just figured they were telling the truth so what's the worst that could really happen? They felt they had no choice in the matter really because they needed to find their friend. The men got back into the truck and drove back to the main road to find a payphone. Remember, it was 1975 and there was no such thing as cellphones for average people, if they even existed back then at all. All of the men were in such a state of shock and panic, literally crying like babies and just completely coming undone; they weren't able to immediately think straight enough to make the call. After debating for a minute or two who was gonna make the call and what they were gonna say, the most level headed of the crew, a man named Ken Peterson is the one who finally made the call to the authorities. He spoke to Sheriff Marlon Gillespie and told him that they couldn't find their friend and while he initially explained what the men were doing in the woods at that hour, that they were working a clearing job, he told the sheriff that he wouldn't be able to explain the course of events over the phone and that the sheriff would have to wait until arriving on scene before he would tell him what happened and why he was calling him at that time in the first place.

CHAPTER 31

TRAVIS WALTON (PART TWO)

A few minutes later Sheriff Gillespie and his partner Ken Copland arrived at the rest stop where the payphone used to call them was located and met the men. They follow the men to the scene and told Ken Peterson, the guy who made the call to them, to start explaining in detail what it was that happened to their friend and how he ended up missing in the forest. Ken being the "level headed one" was trying to stutter out an explanation without using the words "``ufo" or "craft" or "alien" and was obviously having a very hard time in doing so. Those are pretty much the key words needed to accurately describe what the men are claiming happened. Mike Rogers saw his friend struggling to come up with the right words and jumped in, describing the entire scene. He explained about first seeing the UFO and the "lightning" striking Travis and about how they'd all initially fled the scene. Now, obviously the sheriffs are more than skeptical at this point and while the men looked absolutely distressed and terrified and distraught, they were skeptical to say the least about what they were hearing. Gillespie and Copland at this point decided it would be best to search the truck for drugs and/or alcohol, for obvious reasons. They searched the truck and also each individual and found nothing. They also performed field sobriety tests on each of the men just to be sure, and each man, though visibly shaken, seemed to be perfectly sober and not under any kind of influence of alcohol or narcotics. Gillespie, who was in charge, would later state that while he and Copland didn't believe a word of what the men were telling them, they could clearly see that SOMETHING had happened to these men that had put them in a very panicked and shocked state, and so they decided to go ahead and start looking for Travis there in the woods. The reason he so easily went along with this initially was because he actually believed that these men were making up this fantastical story to cover up for the fact that either one or all of them had in fact harmed or killed Travis themselves. He figured once they found Travis, his injuries or whatever else would speak for themselves and the sheriff would then be able to get the real story as to what had gone down from them. So again, he decided to just play along for the moment until he could find Travis or his body and let the evidence speak for itself. He did admit to also thinking that this was the absolute worst cover up story he had ever heard in his entire life, let alone his whole career in law enforcement. A ufo? Yeah right!!

A few hours later when the sun started coming up, there had already been a huge search effort put into place by the sheriff and his partner. The crew themselves, other police officers, hundreds of volunteers, dogs etc. were leaving nothing to chance when it came to finding Travis Walton and in their minds, finding out the real truth of what had happened to or been done to him. After extensively searching for hours though, nobody had come up with anything at all. There was not a single clue or shred of evidence that pointed to Travis's whereabouts. At that point Gillespie and Copland approached the six crew members and started offering deals. They were saying things like, "Just tell us where you hid the body and we'll take it easy on you." and things like that. The men were completely taken aback by this, they knew they hadn't done anything wrong but were getting really scared because they knew how crazy it all sounded. They could feel the pressure and were starting to come to the realization that, if Travis wasn't found soon, they were going to be blamed for murdering him, body or no body. Remember the only "proof" the men had was what they saw and couldn't prove. There was no evidence of any of it anywhere around them either.

The crew members were obviously very worried at that point, not just for Travis now but for themselves. This is when they noticed that, included in the search party were three men. These three men stood out to them because they were uniformly dressed in bright red jackets and they were scanning the ground with tools that somewhat looked to Mike Rogers and the other men like metal detectors, but not. Mike, kind of naively, thought that the three men were some kind of paranormal investigators. I mean, why not right? If there's six men all saying the exact same thing about a UFO zapping their friend and making him basically disappear into thin air, why wouldn't there be some sort of paranormal investigation happening in tandem with the official police search? Mike decided to approach one of the men and asked him what the tool was that he was using. The man responded by telling Mike that he and the other two men were using the tools to test for radiation. Mike continued to ask questions, specifically if the men were with some kind of paranormal research team or if they were with a volunteer organization or were they working for the sheriff's office. The man would only answer with, "we are just checking for radiation" and nothing else. Mike seized the opportunity after realizing that he and the other five crew members were most likely close enough to Travis when the light blasted him that if there was any radiation, they probably were exposed to it as well. He explained that to the man he was speaking to and requested that he scan the whole crew. He asked him to scan their bodies, tools, the truck and all of their clothes. He wanted them to scan anything they could, thinking this might be at least some sort of evidence to stop the sheriff from arresting them for possible murder. When the men obliged and scanned everyone, it all came up negative for radioactivity. That's when Mike, who I'm sure was just absolutely physically and mentally exhausted by that point, remembered that everyone had gone home to shower and change by then. He realized the only thing that they were physically wearing at the time of the event, the only thing that wasn't left home when they all went to shower and change clothes and whatever, were their hard hats. He took one of the hard hats from the back of the work truck and presented it to the strange red jacket guys to be checked for radioactivity. The man scanned it and sure enough, it was off the charts on the testing machine for radioactivity. The guy in red made a silent gesture to the other two men he was seemingly working with who were also "scanning" the area for them to come over. It seemed like an urgent gesture, almost like he was signaling to them something along the lines of, "stop what you're doing and come take a look at this right now!" The other two men came over and both of them scanned the hard hat that Mike gave them and again, on all three of the testing machines the radiation levels were off the charts. The strangest thing though is that after seeing this, the men just turned and walked off to leave. Mike yelled after them, he was obviously expecting some kind of information or explanation or at least to be told what comes next but, all three men continued to just walk off without looking back and without uttering a single word.

The rest of the crew also witnessed this strange exchange between Mike and the red jacket guys and they all decide to approach the sheriffs about what just happened. Now, keep in mind, these men knew with absolute certainty, pretty much bc they were told in no uncertain terms, that the sheriffs believe that they did something to Travis and are making up this insane and frankly unbelievable story as some kind of cover up. However, they approached the sheriffs anyway and asked them who the men in red were and what they were doing at the search site. They asked the sheriff why the men had been testing for radioactivity and also, why they just left the way they did after testing the hard hat. Obviously and for good reason, they wanted answers because this was a very strange exchange and the men had definitely had their fair share of strange for a while with what they saw and what had happened to Travis, right? They went ahead and asked the sheriff those questions and true to form in this already bizarre story, the sheriff had absolutely no idea who or what men they were talking about. Gillespie claimed to have not seen anyone in red with radiation detectors and had no idea why they'd been there or what they'd been testing for. He said he hadn't seen any men like that and had no idea why anyone would have been testing for radioactivity. Gillespie explained, very condescendingly, that he was the one in charge of the investigation and search and the only "official" people who were there were the people he either ordered to be there or invited. Turns out, upon further inquiry by the extremely confused and scared crew members, that nobody at all except for the six of them had even seen those three men, let alone knew who they were, what they were doing and/or why they were allegedly doing it.

The search for Travis went on for a couple of days and yielded absolutely nothing at all. No clues, no evidence and not Travis himself, neither dead nor alive. There was nothing to be found. At that point, it wasn't just the sheriffs and other officials who were accusing the crew members of murdering Travis and basically concocting this entire elaborate and unbelievable hoax just to try and throw everyone off of what they had done, but the town of Snowflake Arizona, where this happened also turned on the men. They felt like these men were wasting the time of the volunteers and the resources of law enforcement with this so-called cover up scheme. Essentially, everyone in the whole town and all of law enforcement wholly believed that these men had done something to, most likely murdered, Travis Walton. The sheriff's office did everything they could to put their opinions out there and all but flat out accused the six men of murder. They did absolutely nothing to stop the perpetuation of these rumors or theories, if that's what you wanna call them. At this point National and International news media had descended upon the small town and picked up the wild story. It was sensational from the very beginning. If they had things go viral back in 1975, this definitely would've been something that did. The papers ran articles like, "Snowflake men claim extraterrestrial abduction" and "Six witnesses passed lie tests while claiming….Arizona man captured by UFO!" Also, "saucers ray struck logger, witnesses say." It was a really big story and the men had been given, and had passed, several lie detector tests by that point. Of course, this fact is what made the story all the more interesting. I wanna talk about the polygraph tests for just a minute.

Sheriff Gillespie, who was the guy in charge of the entire investigation, decided he was being made to look a fool in all of this, especially with all of the media sensationalizing the encounter that he was thoroughly convinced was a cover up for something more sinister. He was thoroughly convinced that this was a murder case and that the men all knew where Travis' body was and were working together not only to get away with it, but to make him look bad personally. Sheriff Gillespie went and hired the country's top and most well respected polygrapher to give the men the tests again. Each crew member was tested that very day, for two hours each, and all of them were asked the same questions. Basically what they did with Travis, what really happened, did they murder him, where was Travis' body etc. Five of the six men passed the lie detector test with flying colors and the sixth person's results were inconclusive. This doesn't mean this last person lied, it simply means the test couldn't determine one way or another whether he was lying or telling the truth. Keep in mind, the polygraph examiner who conducted these tests on the men had a ninety eight percent accuracy rate and was known throughout the country as the best in his field. He himself stated after the results were made public that the odds of five separate men all lying about the same exact thing and passing the same exact questions on a polygraph given the same day by the country's leading polygrapher were astronomical. Basically there was no way it could happen. There is no way the men were lying about what they saw. Some people however, the sheriff included, thought that they may have passed because they actually believed in what they'd reportedly seen, and not because they had actually witnessed it. Like a mass hallucination or mass hysteria I suppose. Gillespie and his partner had no idea where to go from there because they were so sure that this was just all a big hoax, created in order to sow confusion and to cover up a murder, that they wanted nothing more than to just arrest the men and offer them deals in order to get at least one of them to tell what really happened and to lead them to Travis' remains. However, because of the passed polygraphs, that wasn't going to happen. They had no clue what to do next or what their next move was going to be, but they were really angry.

Five days after all of this happened and the men had passed the polygraphs, unbelievably, Travis reappeared! I am about to recount for you what Travis himself said happened to him that night. The first thing he said he remembered was waking up on some sort of road. It was raining and nighttime and he had no clue where he was or which road he was on. He was completely lost on a rainy night on an unknown dark road, somewhere. He was lying face down on the road and said he sensed somehow that an extremely bright light was above him. He turned to look up into the sky and saw a blinding light that was shining and pointed directly down on him from above. He saw what looked to him like the underside of that weird craft he and his coworkers had come across. Although he didn't remember when they'd had that encounter or seen this thing in the sky, he remembered the whole experience. He especially remembered right before he got zapped by the light and blown in the air. He believed that was exactly what he was looking at- the underside of the craft that had him so awestruck he couldn't pull himself away in time and ended up getting thrown fifty feet across the forest while his friends looked on in horror and shock. He saw the ship and though his vision was somewhat blurry at that moment, he knew without a doubt that was what he was seeing. No more than a second after he looked up and realized what it was, it took off in the blink of an eye, upward into the sky and disappeared. It was completely gone not only from his sight but seemingly from the sky as well. When the ship thing took off, it obviously took the light with it and that's when Travis realized whatever road he was on and wherever he was, it was pitch black. The underside of that ship had been the only light for as far as he could see down the road. Travis stood up and that's when he realized he was really weak and dizzy, not feeling very well at all and was pretty sure that he needed to somehow summon the strength to keep walking forward and find someone or some means of help because he was feeling so incredibly depleted of everything at that point. Travis said that he seriously thought he was in danger of collapsing and dying right there on this unknown road in the pitch black dark. While he started off weak and staggering and barely able to take a single step, he chose a direction and somehow, maybe adrenaline or maybe his mind telling him he didn't have much longer and couldn't waste any time, he started running as fast as he could in one direction. After just a few minutes of running he spotted a rest stop up ahead and knew he needed to stop there for some kind of help. Any kind of help, really, because he was feeling like he was gonna die at that point. Travis stopped at the rest stop and decided to use one of the public payphones they had there.

He happened to have some change for the phone in his pocket somehow, honestly, and for some people that's the most unbeliev-able part of this story. Skeptics will always exist I suppose. Travis decided his first call would be to his brother. He realized he knew where he was after all, now that he had a chance to look around the area and rest stop. He recognized that he was back home, in his home town of Snowflake, Arizona. Travis called his brother, who, remember, it's been five days at that point, thinks he's most likely dead. His brother didn't believe at first he was actually speaking to Travis and almost hung up. His brother later said he'd thought that someone was playing some kind of cruel joke on him and his family. It took Travis a few minutes of convincing but finally he got his brother to agree to go and pick him up at the rest stop. Travis said to his brother on the phone, "It's me, it's Travis. They brought me back!" It's important to note that Travis later stated that he thought he had only been gone for a few minutes and didn't understand why his brother was acting the way he was. Actually, Travis wasn't even really sure what had happened and had no immediate memory of being abducted or anything. He was really confused and thought somehow he had been struck by whatever that beam was, and he thought that after being struck he'd simply passed out. He also thought he'd landed on the road he'd just woken up on and didn't realize yet that he'd been dropped off there. I am sure it was hard making sense of all of this at that point. After all, he'd only been awake at that point for a few minutes, just long enough to find his way to a payphone and get his brother on the line. His brother finally realized he was indeed speaking to Travis and hurried to go and picked him up from the rest stop. Travis immediately got into his brother's car. This is when his brother tells him how worried sick everyone was and how they all thought he was dead. His brother also explained to him that after all this time they really thought they were never gonna see him again. It was at this point Travis finally understood how long he'd been gone. Travis stated that the minute he heard he had been missing for five days it was like his mind had finally given up trying to understand anything and he went into a state of shock. He was almost to the point of being catatonic. His mind probably couldn't handle anymore. Just because the memories were hidden at that point doesn't mean they weren't in there somewhere and that he hadn't just gone through whatever it was that he had gone through. It was all too much and Travis' mind basically started shutting down while right there in the car with his brother. His brother was still trying to get an answer out of him as to what happened but Travis was completely unable to answer and just sat there, as I said, pretty much catatonic and unable to move or speak. His brother was extremely concerned about him, both his physical and also his mental health seemed to be in some trouble. His brother decided that taking Travis to a hospital first would be the best thing. He considered that, if the media gets a hold of the news that Travis has returned, which was almost guaranteed if he brought him to the police station, then Travis may have not been able to handle it. His brother wanted to make sure Travis was taken care of above all else and he knew that the media and the police each had their own agenda and Travis's best interest wasn't it for either party. They made their way to the hospital.

CHAPTER 32
TRAVIS WALTON (PART THREE)

Travis's brother decided to bring him to a hospital in Phoenix Arizona and once they got there he asked the staff to please be discreet in handling the situation because his brother seemed very disturbed and in a bad way. He could tell right away that everyone knew who Travis was and that he'd been missing and presumed murdered for the last five days. During Travis' examination the doctor noticed he was obviously tired, but also dehydrated and malnourished as well. Basically, he was extremely weak. The only visible "wound" on Travis's body however was a single needle puncture site in the crook of his arm, on the inside of his elbow. Travis didn't use drugs and especially not intravenous drugs so that was not a reasonable explanation for the mark on his arm there. It was an unexplained wound but of course the doctor wasn't going to just take his word for it and decided to see for himself if he could find an explanation for the needle mark, like certain substances coming up in toxicology results. The doctor ran multiple kinds of drug tests (blood, urine etc.) and everything came up negative. The next reasonable assumption, at least in Travis' mind, was that someone else had recently punctured his skin with a needle. Whether someone would have done that to inject him with something or withdraw something from him he wasn't sure and in fact he wasn't much sure of anything at that point in time. Each thought was more horrific than the next and everyone involved there at the hospital last night was really confused and freaked out. Travis was for the most part given a clean bill of health except for some minor things like needing to sleep, eat and drink.

After he was released from the hospital just a few hours later, Travis and his brother went to the brother's house there in Phoenix, Arizona. No sooner did the two men walk through the front door of the brother's home than the phone started ringing. It rang almost non-stop from that point on. It was apparent to both men that the word had leaked out about Travis' miraculous return. They eventually received a call from Sheriff Gillespie back at the Snowflake Sheriff's Department and they're asked if Sheriff Gillespie could come to the brother's home and interview Travis right away. He didn't think it would be a good idea for his brother to leave the home or to be seen anywhere out in public and since they still didn't really understand who (or what) they were dealing with, Travis was actually afraid to leave the home at all as well. When the sheriff saw Travis he realized how terrible he looked and he would later say that it was obvious to him that Travis had been through some kind of serious ordeal. Sheriff Gillespie was eager to ask Travis what everyone else wanted to know and he wasted no time in doing so once he was inside of the house with him. He asked, "Where have you been all of this time and what happened to you?" Travis couldn't really remember much at that point but he told the sheriff that he remembered seeing a craft, a "ufo" in the clearing and getting out of the work truck to get a better look at it. He stated that he was admiring the craftsmanship of the underside of the ship and was suddenly struck by a beam of light that literally lifted him off the ground and blew him back about fifty feet. However, Travis stated the next thing he remembered was waking up face down on a strange road, in the rain, with the craft hovering above him, completely disorientated and confused. He told the rest of the story of what happened up until that point and that was it. Sheriff Gillespie didn't know what to think or believe but, it seemed there was nothing criminal going on aside from maybe a waste of police and volunteer resources. He couldn't arrest Travis either because there was no way to prove or disprove at that point in time whether or not what Travis was saying was true. The sheriff told Travis to rest up and not to leave town and then he left the brother's home not knowing what to think, what to believe, or even what in the world was to be done about it.

After the sheriff finally left, news media started showing up in roves outside of Travis' brother's home. Huge news vans,cameras and reporters, all basically camped out on the brother's front yard trying to get an interview with Travis or at the very least to get some questions answered for a story to run. They needed something to tell the public and the world, both of whom were following this story so closely. The National Enquirer reached out and offered to pay for Travis and his brother to go somewhere where nobody would be able to find them while Travis went for another whole battery of tests, both for his mind and body, including hypnosis which they also offered to pay for. Of course, they'd do all of that in exchange for an exclusive story. The brothers decided that this was the best offer and the best chance not only for Travis to be able to rest up and start trying to be and feel normal again, but to find out what had actually happened to him. They accepted the offer and gave the Enquirer the exclusive story they'd been seeking. The magazine did as promised and brought him and his brother to a private hide out spot where he could just relax and rest without everyone hounding him for answers he didn't even have.. Yet.

When Travis was finally put in the "safe house" he was able to relax a bit more and he also had time to finally think about exactly what had happened to him that night. From the time of getting zapped by the beam of light to waking up on the wet and cold ground in the darkness five nights later, he knew there had to be so much more in-between that he was missing. As he sat down for his first interview with the National Enquirer he began to get flashes of memory of what happened. This was the first time this had happened to him but he'd also had plenty of time to rest and recuperate before the interview took place. He started to tell the interviewer what he remembered. Here is what Travis had to say; He started at the beginning and stated that he remembers getting out of the truck and walking towards the strange craft while the other guys yelled for him to stop and come back to the truck. He remembered being kind of awestruck by the sight of the under-side of it. He stated that right as he started to turn around and head back to the truck, the craft started spinning and emitting an extremely loud noise and that's when the beam of light shot out of the bottom of it and zapped him. After this he said he remem-bered seeing an extremely bright white light, and he saw as well what he thought to be doctors. These "doctors" even had on white lab coats and facial coverings, kind of like surgical masks. It all seemed very ordinary despite the extraordinary way he had come to be in the presence of these "doctors". His immediate reaction was that he was in the hospital because whatever had zapped him from that ship had caused him some kind of injury, at least a black out, because he couldn't remember being transported to this "hos-pital" at all. These were seemingly perfectly reasonable thoughts and assumptions up to this point from Travis. He was in and out of consciousness at that point but he recalled being aware, as he faded in and out, that he was around who he believed to be medical professionals. He was very adamant about that point and that might be to explain why he wasn't yet panicked in any way. Basically, he'd been comforted a bit by those thoughts. He stated that he once again woke up and instead of having blurry and kinda foggy vision, he could see everything completely. This is when the seriousness of his situation, and the terror, began for him.

Travis noticed that there was a rectangular box sitting on his chest. He said he had only just recognized that it was there and wasn't sure if it had been there all along, meaning all of the other times he'd woken up and passed back out again, or if this box was a new addition to the scene unfolding in front of him. He didn't recognize it at all and had no idea how long it had been there either. He stated that he'd never seen anything like it before and had only referred to it as a box because of the shape of it. He noticed the rock-like rectangular box sitting on his chest and he looked up and saw that one of the "doctors" was working on or doing something with the box. The "doctor" then leaned in and took a closer look at Travis, almost as if to check and make sure he was actually awake with his eyes open. However, when this "doctor" did this he leaned in so very close, and that's when Travis noticed it wasn't a doctor at all. In fact, it wasn't even human! The creature had huge black shiny eyes, all black, and it stood at about four feet tall. Travis was terrified beyond words and said it just kept dawning on him, over and over again, that this thing wasn't a human person, it wasn't a human doctor, and in fact everything about the creature and his situation was inhuman. This is the point where he'd completely lost it and started tearing the whole room up. He ripped out all the cords attached to him and pulled off any kind of machinery he could get his hands on. Anything attached to his body, basically, he started ripping and tearing at and throwing as he tried to jump up off of the table he'd been lying on. It dawned on him as he did this that the table had been very similar to our operating tables here on Earth. As Travis continued to panic, he looked around and saw that the being who was working on him wasn't alone and there were two more of them there in the tiny room he was in. Travis picked up the first "weapon" he could find which was one of the weird and unknown instruments that were lying on a table next to where he'd just been. He didn't know what it was that he was wielding but he started doing exactly that, he started chopping and stabbing at the air, trying to ward off any approach by these humanoid creatures he's encountered. He was also screaming at the top of his voice for them to stay back and not to come any closer to him. He was in full blown panic mode and I can honestly say I don't blame him one little bit. This, however, does nothing to deter the figures from approaching him. They slowly walked towards him, in a somewhat straight line and they were silent the entire time, looking like they were just as confused as he was about what's going on here. It was almost like they hadn't expected Travis to flip out and become violent the way he had. One of them actually managed to get close enough where he came within about a millimeter from getting whacked with whatever Travis had grabbed off of the table. All of the sudden though, all three creatures abruptly stopped dead in their tracks and turned and walked out of the room, leaving Travis scared and in a panic holding some unknown instrument or object in his hand.

Travis followed them all to the door and looked out to see which direction the beings had gone in and he kept his eyes directly on their backs as they walked away to see exactly where they were going. He watched them until they disappeared around a corner. Although he was admittedly almost to the point of being paralyzed with fear, Travis must've had some of his wits about him because he realized that this was his chance to get out of that room and try to maybe get away from those things and also get the hell out of there. Those beings, when they left that room, didn't close the door or lock him in or anything! Travis had seen that they'd all turned left around the corner after walking through a little hallway so he walked into the same hallway but turned right. He ended up in another tiny little room but this one only had one single chair in it and nothing else. He saw that the chair was empty and walked past it. He started touching all over all of the walls, trying to see if there was some way out of that room, out of wherever he was. He was desperate and determined to get himself out of there and away from those creatures. However, Travis was unsuccessful in finding a way out through the walls. He did turn and saw there were some buttons on the chair so he examined those to see if he could figure out what any of them were. He once again had no luck, even after pressing every single button on the chair multiple times. Just as he looked up at the door to try and figure out another escape plan, he saw a man. There was an actual human being, a man, standing in the doorway staring at him.

Imagine Travis' relief when he saw an actual person! He figured that this person would be able to help him get the hell out of there, wherever it was he'd found himself anyway, he still didn't know. The man was wearing what looked to Travis like one of those space suits astronauts wear when they go into outer space. Like what Neil Armstrong was wearing when he went to the moon. Travis ran over to the man who was wearing the space suit and started pleading for help and asking where they were. He assumed this human would not only help him to get out of wherever he was and away from those creature things but also that he would have at least some form of answers for him. Travis was wrong, however, because this is when he noticed that the man had a very strange look about him. His eyes were very unfocused and although he seemed to be looking at Travis, he actually wasn't. It was like he wasn't actually seeing anything that was in front of him. Travis said the look was an unfocused and/or glazed over kind of look. It didn't make him feel any better, or any safer. The strange man turned to walk out of the room and Travis followed him because although the guy was obviously very weird and had some issues, seemingly, it was another human and Travis had to hold onto that thought to get himself through all of this. The man opened and walked through a door and Travis dutifully followed. As Travis followed the strange man out of the room and down another hallway, he asked some questions. He had to repeat the questions multiple times and he was asking things like, "what's going on?" "where are we?" "what was that thing?" etc. However, it quickly became apparent that the space suit guy either couldn't or wouldn't speak. That didn't stop Travis from asking though because his adrenaline was obviously spiked at that moment.

As they walked down another long corridor, Travis remembered seeing a lot of other crafts. All of them were exactly like the one that Travis and the crew saw; the one that zapped him. Some were just as large, some were smaller and there were a few that were several sizes in between. Despite being fairly confident that the space guy wasn't going to answer him, he asked some questions anyway. He figured at that point he really didn't have anything to lose and he didn't feel as terrified with the human-looking man as he had when he was surrounded by the strange little creatures. He asked things like, "what are these?" "where are we? "who are you?" Again though, just as he'd expected, he received absolutely nothing, not even a grunt in response. Eventually Travis ended up following this "man" into yet another room. This room however was very brightly lit, almost like the room he'd originally woken up in. He looked ahead and saw three more "humans". They were all the exact same as the other man though, the original one he'd been following around. They looked different from him as far as features and all of that, like every human is different, however, they all had that same, weird, kind of far away look going on with them, in their eyes too. They were also wearing the same space suits as man number one. As Travis and the first "human guy" walked into this room, the three other "men" turned as though they were looking at them, but oddly enough, they only turned their bodies to face Travis. He said it seemed as though they were staring blankly somewhere beyond him. Travis said he felt such relief again because he once again thought these "people" were there to save him, to help him in some way. The human things approached Travis and took him by the arms, leading him towards another operating table. At first Travis allowed himself to be led but upon realizing they intended to put him on the table, he started resisting. It was pointless because he was very quickly overcome and forced to lie on the table anyway. The men held him down while one of them placed what looked like some sort of gas mask on his face. Travis immediately blacked out. The very next thing he remembered was waking up face down in the rain on that lonely and dark stretch of road.

Travis was so busy helping with the "police investigation" and doing interviews and telling his story that it took him a while to meet up and reconnect with the other men who were there with him the night he was abducted. Eventually though, the men and Travis met at Mike Rogers' house and Travis told them the story of what happened. They all immediately believed him despite not wanting to. After leaving Mike's house that day, all seven of the men went their own way. They didn't stay in touch or really ever speak to each other again. Even today, more than forty five years later, when they do an interview or speak about that night, they always end up extremely emotional and in tears. The crew members carry around a lot of guilt because they wonder if, had they just stayed and immediately went to help him, would Travis have been spared this entire ordeal? There's no way of knowing that though, and in my opinion, what I tend to believe is that Travis would've been taken either way. However, there's obviously no way of really knowing if it would've made any kind of difference. What if somehow they all would've ended up missing for a few days, abducted? Speaking of when the men do interviews now, Ken Peterson's interviews are particularly hard for me to watch. He's an older man now and Ken says that to this very day and probably until the day he dies, he is now and always will be afraid to even just look out of his window. The man never stopped living in absolute terror of these things. Who knows, maybe he thinks they're gonna come back for him or something? It's hard to watch for sure, to see a grown man cry and just seem so fragile and small because of his palpable fear when talking about this event. Despite being labeled as "the most credible UFO abduction story", the actual truth is that this has affected these men's lives in very negative ways. Their credibility was ruined, they couldn't find employment, people were always looking at them strangely and pointing at them.

I couldn't find much information on any of the men that were there that night. I know Travis is very public about his experience and attends UFO conferences and doesn't usually pass up an opportunity to tell the story. He says it's because people are afraid to speak out about being abducted and he wants to show them it's ok and people need to be made aware of these things. I did find out that one of the men changed his name and went into hiding and didn't resurface until thirty years after the incident, about fifteen years ago. The area of the abduction was burned by a fire in 2002 and the access road the men were on has been decommissioned by the forest service. It came out several years ago too that there was a group of hunters in those same woods on the night Travis was abducted who had actually seen the lights of the craft. In more than forty years none of these men ever changed their story at all about what happened that night. More than a dozen lie detector tests have been collectively passed by them in that time as well. The odds of this being a hoax, in my opinion and just taking the passed polygraphs as evidence, the odds have to be astronomical! I often wonder where non-believers and skeptics think Travis was for those five days and six hours if not on a spaceship, off of this earth, and being subject to torturous procedures by extraterrestrial entities. For me, anything other than what Travis said is exactly what happened would be too much of a stretch of the imagination for me to make and I just can't fathom it being a hoax.

CHAPTER 33
ACAPULCO ABDUCTION

At two am on a dark morning in January of 1954, a man named Armando Zubaran was in his car and driving along the winding, desolate roads on his way from Mexico City to Acapulco, Mexico. Armando was meeting up with a business partner later in the morning and he more than likely was kicking himself for putting himself in the position to have to drive such a perilous journey in the middle of the night. The roads were rugged, twisting and meandering through all sorts of switchbacks and mountain passes and he knew he had to give every bit of attention to the road ahead of him or else he could end up with something bad happening to him. All he could see, on that dark road in the middle of the night, were the white lines down the middle, flashing before him in his headlights. Armando later said that he was fully awake and not tired at all for the entire trip as he'd been well rested in preparation for the meeting. However, all of the sudden an intense tiredness befell him and he referred to this as "a hypnotic state of lethargy." This was how one of the most bizarre, though also somehow mostly forgotten, alien abductions on record began.

The lethargy that hit him out of the blue had him almost falling asleep at the wheel. Despite being confused as to where it came from in the first place, Armando had the presence of mind to know that he couldn't continue driving in such hazardous conditions being as tired as he was. He pulled his vehicle over to the side of the road, intending to relax for a couple of minutes, before returning to the road and continuing on his journey. As he sat there, he suddenly started to notice something strange ahead of him in the distance.There, hovering right over the middle of that remote mountain road before him, Armando saw what looked to be a luminous, very brightly lit metallic disc of some kind, but when he tried harder to peer into the light to see what the source of it was, he noticed only that he was no longer out there alone. Standing on each side of the strange object were two very tall figures, and they both seemed to be dressed in the same one piece suit cinched with wide belts in the middle. They appeared to have had long, flowing hair, and for a minute or so they merely stood there, almost completely obscured by the incredibly bright glow emanating from the strange disc-shaped object. Armando didn't understand what was happening and sat there trying to determine what was going on and also trying to figure out what to do next. However, that didn't last long because he was suddenly compelled to exit the vehicle. He wasn't only compelled, and in fact he said he was overtaken, with him feeling as though he had no control at all over his own limbs. He was exiting the vehicle and walking towards the tall figures, but he had no control over doing so. Things only got more bizarre from there.

As he got closer to the figures, he saw that they both appeared to be male, but he clarified that they mainly just looked androgynous. He also described them as looking almost like normal humans and "Nordic looking", with blonde hair and blue eyes. The two beings moved quickly to help Armando steady himself as whatever had been controlling his limbs up to that point had let him go and he was dazed and weak because of it. The two figures then started to escort him towards their ship, which he could clearly see was in fact a ship at that point. As all of this was going on a buzzing noise, intense and headache inducing, filled his head. Once he was aboard the brightly glowing ship he looked around and then almost immediately asked the beings what they wanted with him and why he'd been brought there. One of the strange, blonde beings replied to him, in perfectly fluent Spanish, "You are neither the first nor last earthman to be chosen for testing. Our task, slow though it may seem, is designed to persuade. We choose the likeliest, most malleable persons for contact, so that they might better transmit our messages." Armando had no idea what to make of that statement and didn't have time to process any of what was happening or what had just been said to him because right after the one being spoke to him, the two of them immediately started to show him a series of images from his own life. The images were shown to him as they played like a projector movie over a wall in the ship. He later explained that some of the images they had shown him were from very intimate times in his life and some of it was things he'd forgotten, somehow dug up from the corners of his mind where memories go to die. It suddenly dawned on Armando that these creatures had either gone into his mind in order to project the images or that they'd been watching and following him for a very long time, perhaps most of his life. The images stopped just as suddenly as they'd begun and then he was shown around the ship, which he was informed was no longer on the ground and no longer even on Earth anymore at that point. That information startled Armando because as far as he could tell the craft never moved at all and had seemingly been still the entire time he'd been on it. No sense of movement or acceleration had been evident in the slightest, and when he asked about it, he was told that they used something called a "gravity repulsion system" but they never elaborated further as to what that was, exactly. They did tell him that they were able to neutralize any debris in their path or anything that got in the way of their travels, and when they instructed him to look out of a portal he wasn't able to see anything but some gray mist standing out only a little from the sea of darkness surrounding it.

Armando became even more curious and asked the entities if they were traveling to their home planet, wherever that was, but they told him that wasn't where they were going and for several days they seemingly just roamed around in outer space. During those few days Armando became aware of how the ship worked, and he spent a lot more time with his bizarre and mysterious captors. He later admitted he was perplexed by a lot of things on the ship and their way of living on it, but the bathroom facilities are what confused him the most. I thought at first that this meant actually going to the bathroom, as in using the toilet or something but that wasn't what Armando had meant. He described it himself, the showering process, by saying, "I shall never be able to forget it. That bathroom was a new and unimaginable experience for me. Standing upright, facing an angle of the wall filled with tiny holes, I was covered in warm air, and as it grew stronger, it became transformed into damp air, impregnating my skin like a warm, wet breeze. When I was completely drenched, I was offered a sort of liquid soap, which I rubbed all over myself, from head to toe. Standing once more before the warm air sprinklers, I felt the soap begin to evaporate and my skin become completely clean. The air then ceased to be damp, turning dry and warm instead of becoming colder until agreeably cool." That actually sounds really cool and quite lovely to be honest.

Of course he had to eat while he was with them and he described their food as being a lot like what we eat here on earth. They ate meat, vegetables, cheese and even butter. Though he said it was similar, he also said it was nothing at all like what we have on earth and for me that just meant it was more than likely much better quality and unlike anything he had ever tasted or even seen before, but that he knew what it was by what it looked like. The food was almost always accompanied by a milky liquid that the aliens told him was made of materials from their own home and was their main form of sustenance. They told him they utilized many fruits and vegetables grown on earth, with mangoes being one of their favorites. Mangoes specifically featured heavily in their diet and it almost seemed like the beings couldn't get enough of them. The extraterrestrials told Armando that they got the food aboard the ship by beaming it from the ground or wherever it was at the time directly into the ship itself. They used an outside source similar to telepathy to do this and they did so whenever it was necessary. Armando had many discussions with the aliens and he learned that their average life span was two hundred and fifty years! They explained to him that on their planet and in their society, everyone was treated equally. There was no such thing as hate or cruelty there. In fact, they told him as well that their whole way of life was based on their own religious beliefs. Those beliefs included a being whom they called "the master" or "the beloved number nine" and it had governed them for thousands of years. It also kept them safe and their society peaceful and running smoothly.

After their time together was over, Armando was simply brought back to earth. He was unceremoniously dropped back off at his car, which was still sitting in the exact same spot just as he'd left it several days earlier. Armando said goodbye to them and then figured the only thing he could do was continue on his way to Acapulco, but he soon realized something shocking. The several days he had been gone only amounted to an hour and a half here on Earth. He had only technically been gone, at least for all intents and purposes, for ninety minutes! In fact, he ended up making it to his business meeting on time. Making this whole thing even stranger, at least for some, is the fact that fifteen years later in 1969 Armando would once again be traveling outside of Mexico City when he stopped to pick up a hitchhiker who was a tall, thin man with long and flowing blonde hair and bright blue eyes. The hitchhiker eventually admitted that he was indeed a crew member on the ship that Armando had been on years earlier and though he obviously had a purpose for being on the side of the road that day, Armando never discussed further what they talked about or why the being was there to see him. At least that's how Armando tells the story, but many people, myself included, have a hard time believing nothing else was said about the experience or anything else about the previous abduction carried out on him.

Throughout the 1950s, when all of this originally happened, there would be numerous other reports of people coming into contact with these "Nordic aliens." In every report, just as in Armando's, they appear to be very tall and thin, with long and flowing blonde hair and unusually bright blue eyes. They're also always described as being "angelic looking." It's hard not to wonder if maybe they were all connected somehow, but of course there's no way we could ever know that. Some people believe that what we now refer to as the Nordic aliens are literal angels from heaven but in my estimation that's ridiculous. I feel that way for reasons I won't bore you with here, and everyone is of course entitled to think what they want. After all, none of us really knows anything for sure anyway. Of course there are skeptics out there who say this was all merely a made up and fantastical story told by a man who was bored in life and perhaps needed a reason as to why he was late for a meeting. Most reports say he arrived on time, though admittedly there are a couple that claim he was a little late in meeting that businessman. Whether or not this is a true story I can't prove to you all one way or another and you have to make up your own minds about that, like with everything else in this book. I will say that I believe it's true and in fact I believe in most alien abduction encounters because in my experience you never really know what's going on in someone else's life and I would never want to discount someone who has had such an experience. For as incredible as these usually are, most abductions are not something happy and exciting and in fact are painful and cause lots of psychological and emotional trauma. I like to err on the side of caution and give people the benefit of the doubt, just as I always do with paranormal experiences as well. The main thing about this case that stood out to me was the fact that it involved the Nordic aliens as they are not at all the entities I tend to think of when I think about abduction experiences. However, in researching for this book, I came to realize they're a lot more common than most people think they are.

CHAPTER 34
DULCE BASE

Our next case is a little different and starts in a very small town in New Mexico which has an almost science fiction like story surrounding it. It's at the very heart of the "aliens could very well be eating us" declaration too. As I've said a few times in this book already, does anyone really know the truth anyway? No- but that shouldn't make us immediately dismiss anything as crazy or too outlandish. After all, let's stay cognizant of the subject matter at hand in the first place right? It's said that there were some deliberate things done and tactics put in place both in the mid seventies and again in the mid nineties to purposely confuse the UFO research community and the public as a whole and to make it so most of us don't even consider that this could be going on. Let's talk about the town of Dulce, New Mexico and what allegedly goes on there in the secret underground base no one is supposed to know about.

Dulce is in Rio Arriba County and is a very small town of approximately three thousand residents. It's thirteen square miles around and it's the home of the Jicarilla Apache Nation. Dulce was founded in the later part of the nineteenth century and is, seemingly at least upon first glance, almost boringly ordinary. Take a closer look though and you may be shocked and possibly frightened at what you will see. Since the late 1970s there have been rumors circulating around this tiny town that would make your head spin and your stomach turn if you even entertain the notion of believing in them. It's been alleged that deep within the Archuletta Mesa, which admittedly takes up most of the town's square mileage, there lay a very futuristic, and very secret, underground facility, or lair if you want to put it that way, that even the United States main government entities aren't privy to or even the slightest bit aware of. It's said even today that these particular subterranean quarters are under the complete and total control of a very hostile and very dangerous group of extraterrestrials. The aliens who are said to have domination over not only the seven story tall base, which is completely and totally hidden underground, are what we have come to know as the small grays. These dwarfish creatures have giant black eyes that are often described as being soulless and extremely large heads. These are the aliens who would more than likely pop into most of our population's mind when someone mentions the words alien abduction. In all the research I've done and have been doing for years on end now, I find that these aliens are the ones who are abducting human beings nine times out of ten or more.

Legend has it that in 1979 an all out war broke out between the aliens and military personnel. It was a violent confrontation and the human beings were the ones who lost. It's claimed the base was a giant place where humans and aliens interacted and worked together on a daily basis. It was explained as though, to the human personnel with high enough clearances to have access to this underground base, it was like just another day at the office once they swiped their ID and clearance badges and started their work for the day. However, after this battle where there were many human casualties, the extraterrestrials took over the place. There are some witnesses who came forward, mostly anonymously for fear of the very real threat of losing their lives and possibly the lives of their family and loved ones for their disclosure of such top secret military secrets, and they claim that there were dozens upon dozens of rooms across seven stories and literal caverns where human beings were now being held for experimentation by the extraterrestrials. Also, allegedly, the humans were being served up as a menu option for their snacks and meals. They were said to be devouring the human beings who were left working there or trapped down there after that battle in 1979. Many of the humans who worked there when all of that was happening were said to never have been seen again by anyone outside of the others who were trapped underground in the base with them. So, is this all true and where did these stories come from? I'll tell you what I know to the best of my ability of what I could find in my research. It wasn't easy because a lot of it has been embellished for dramatic flair since the invention of the internet and also, how society views ufology and so-called whistleblowers now. It's such a welcome topic that anyone will come out of the woodwork and say literally anything to get attention and possibly even a book deal. In my opinion anyway.

There was a company in the seventies called Thunder Scientific and it was run by a man named Paul Bennewitz and I decided we should start there if we are going to try and get to the truth of this matter. This company was located in Albuquerque and more specifically was backed right up against the extremely well guarded and super secretive Kirtland Air Force Base. It was a year before the alleged battle that Paul began to start hearing the rumors of possible UFO sightings and ET abductions in, near and around the Albuquerque area. He'd already had a keen interest in the whole world of extraterrestrials, as taboo and unaccepted as it was at the time, and he took even more of an interest when he heard of such things happening right around where his business was located. Late into the night and in the very early hours of the morning, Paul started to notice more and more, strange looking non-military aircraft flying over the base. Paul also kept some sort of radio equipment and at the same time as he was seeing these crafts, he was picking up some rather strange frequencies and signals. Once he started asking questions, and he was getting all types of interesting answers by way of accounts by people in Albuquerque and to the north of their alleged abductions and sightings and radio signals being picked up just like his, he was picked up by unnamed intelligence officers who worked for an unknown branch of either military or the government and he was grilled about what he knew.

He reported later on that their main concern seemed to be the growing number of alleged abductees in the area and what he may have known or came across about that specific topic. The claims were that these people were actually being kidnapped and experimented upon in some of the most bizarre and horrific ways imaginable. More specifically, most of the experimentation is said to have been in the nature of genetics. Once he convinced these men that he knew nothing other than the rumor and speculation that everyone else was hearing he was let go. He continued his research and asking around about what could possibly be going on. He didn't let up and it became somewhat of an obsession for him at the time. The conclusion he came to may sound bizarre, especially considering what we think we know about ETs today and their purpose here. Paul believed that a race of extremely bloodthirsty and violent extraterrestrials were getting ready to take over earth and enslave the human race. He somehow determined they were going to do this from their underground lair that lay right below Dulce military base. No word on how he figured this out or what his thought process was that led him to that conclusion but there it is. That's when he put together his dossier on everything he found and thought. Every piece and scrap of information he had on all of this was put together and organized and he called it Project Beta. He then got to work, and remember this was 1978, mailing copy after copy of this gigantic report to the CIA, the FBI and the NSA. He seriously believed the end was getting nearer and nearer as each day passed and that human enslavement was imminent and right around the corner. He mailed those documents to every single military branch and base in the country. He even mailed a copy to the White House.

In those documents, Paul wrote that the public and people everywhere had to be warned immediately! Despite the time and how we know in most cases someone like this would be written off, the opposite happened and Paul Bennewitz was actually able to establish a secret partnership and contact with intelligence agents at Kirtland Air Force Base. He was not only told by those agents, off the record of course, that he was indeed on the right track but also warned that he needed to immediately stop his research and fade back into the background as quietly as possible or his life and the lives of those he loved could and most likely would be at risk. These kind of veiled and quiet threats to keep his mouth shut and move along like a good little citizen only made him more eager to get to the bottom of things and to warn the American public and possibly even the world at any cost and as soon as possible. The intelligence at Kirtland were almost laughing at him, begging him to just shut up already. Paul didn't listen and he had no intention of stopping. Some of the agents were happy he was doing what he was doing, though they thought it was perhaps a bit stupid and that he was gambling with his life. Despite how they felt, they continued to tell him more and more about what was really going on. He was getting fed information from some of those agents about what was happening underneath the base in Dulce. One of these bits of information was that the extraterrestrials were holding thousands of people captive down there and literally eating them. Paul started becoming paranoid and a bit crazed after hearing all of this. I don't really blame him. After all, these reports weren't coming from your average people off the streets or even alleged abductees but from actual government officials who had the clearance to know what they were talking about.

Unfortunately, and I say that not only because it's a shame when something like this happens to anyone but also because of what it ended up doing to his credibility and in turn to the community here at large, Paul became so unhinged and maniacal about his beliefs and thoughts and truths, he ended up being hospitalized in a psych ward in a nearby hospital. He had a complete mental breakdown and was treated for extreme stress and major anxiety. Go figure! Paul eventually recovered while in the hospital but once he got out he was a changed man. He kept as far away as he could from anything having to do with extraterrestrials, Dulce base and UFOlogy in general. He had finally given up, for fear of losing his sanity- let alone his life. As he got older and right up to his last days alive, Paul wasn't sure if he was being given some misinformation to force him into a mental breakdown so he would stop searching for answers or if he had been told what was really happening in true confidence and just couldn't handle it. This is where Paul's story, and its place in this book, ends. However, I will say this- a man named Phil Schneider eventually came along, allegedly a year later after Paul was first let on to what may be going on under Dulce and he said he was a part of that battle. He also said he saw these aliens eating human beings, including infants and pregnant women. He was murdered by the government, allegedly and it was made to look like he had done it to himself. That's the rumor about Phil anyway.

CHAPTER 35
DANNY CASOLARO

Our next case is about a writer whose name was Danny Casolaro. Between the late eighties and the early nineties, Danny was very vocal about being on the trail of something or someone he referred to as "the octopus." He said it was a worldwide organization with "tentacles" everywhere that manipulated events, made murders look like the person had done it to themselves and he even said that this organization was setting up for all of us to be under the thumb of some sort of new world order in the coming decades. Casolaro also claimed that this "octopus" organization also had some of its tentacles in the field of UFOlogy. On August 1,1991 in a room at the Sheraton Inn in Martinsburg, West Virginia the body of an unknown man was found dead in the shower. By all appearances the man had ended his own life. Deep gashes were found in both his wrists and without anyone around to help him out, as he was allegedly traveling alone, he was left there to just bleed out. Now, if someone were going to kill themselves, I guess this would make sense, that they wouldn't want to be where anyone could get to them and offer any sort of life saving assistance but that's just it isn't it? It wraps up a little too neat for a man who had his whole life ahead of him and truly thought he was onto something groundbreaking.

Hotel staff figured out who he was within just a few minutes of finding him, as he was identified by the person who was working at the front desk of the hotel when he'd checked in. Danny was registered under his real name and was known to be an investigative journalist with a lot of grit who didn't want to keep many secrets. Of course, his friends and loved ones were absolutely devastated and shocked at the news of what had happened to him. Obviously, the person taking their own life isn't the only one who suffers and often it's those who are left behind to pick up the pieces and with so many questions who are victims as well. I agree with that statement wholeheartedly and one hundred percent but let's take a closer look here. Was Danny's death really done by his own hands? It's said that only conspiracy theorists look at this clear cut case of suicide and think it to be something else but I'm not so sure about that. What brought most people into it, myself included, was the UFO angle to the whole thing. Danny said that he had indisputable proof of the existence of the secret group known as The Majestic Twelve. In case you don't know what that is, let me summarize here for you.

The Majestic Twelve, also known as MJ-12 for short, is only an alleged group still to this day and many people write it off as conspiracy theorist jargon. They're said to be a top secret committee of government agents, scientists, military leaders and government officials, that were formed under the executive order of president Truman in 1947 to facilitate recovery and investigations into alien spacecrafts. The concept started circulating among the masses when a series of government documents were allegedly leaked and circulated by ufologists back in 1948. Supposedly it oversaw all of Area 51 and the wreckages and alien bodies that were said to have been found on the night of that infamous crash in the summer of 47 in Roswell, New Mexico. The Majestic Twelve has been a topic of discussion that has been integral to the field of ufology for decades now and for many people who investigate these types of things as well as for a great deal of professionals in the field, the Majestic Twelve is absolutely real.

One other thing I will say before leaving it up in the air, is that just as many people believe it's just some more smoke and mirror information put out into the general public by government officials themselves, in order to further confuse us all about the Roswell incident.

Danny said that he had undeniable evidence and proof that the Majestic Twelve existed and he wasn't planning on keeping it to himself or being quiet about it. By early 1991 he could barely contain himself and for good reason; was excited and adamant about being the one to publicly reveal the existence of "the octopus." However, his death in August of that year ensured that at the very least he wouldn't be the one who put the information out there. As it stands, right now in October of 2025, we still don't have any evidence or definitive proof about the Majestic Twelve one way or another so if this was done to him and for those reasons, it was effective. While his death certainly looked like he had done it himself, there were some very valid and solid reasons as to why that wasn't the case. It's said by everyone who knew him that he wasn't experiencing any sort of overwhelming sadness or depression and was in fact excited about his findings and his life in general. It's said it was actually the exact opposite of anything like that with people saying all of the new leads he was investigating were invigorating and energizing him, as well as his being in positive spirits about his quest to bring the entity he called the octopus, its activities and motivations and any and all new information about it, to the public's attention. He was going to expose some very high up people in the government and he wasn't going to back down. That right there is exactly why many people believe he was murdered and therefore, silenced.

CHAPTER 36
MIRIAM BUSH

In being on the subject of strange deaths in the field of UFOlogy and particularly the Roswell incident, I decided to include another strange death in this book and the theories are similar to those in the previous case we just discussed here. First, let's briefly discuss July of 1947 and what happened in the desert in Roswell, New Mexico. Miriam Bush was someone who knew everything that happened, and what really went down, on that night and in the days and weeks afterwards. It's said she knew so much, in fact, that she more than likely paid for that information with her own life. I just want to set the record straight here because I am always seeing Miriam described as a nurse who worked at the military hospital at the Roswell Army Air Field, but that wasn't the case. She was actually an executive secretary at that same facility. I know it seems like a small distinction and though I did bring it up in part to lend more respect to her memory, it's actually a very important detail that is so often overlooked. With the actual position she held there, she would have had access to and been in a position to view firsthand any and all parts and pieces of the wreckage as it was secretly brought onto the base, right into where she worked, on that night- including any possible mangled bodies, alien or otherwise, that went through there.

It's no secret that immediately following the Roswell crash, Miriam was said to have become extremely paranoid and lived in constant fear for her life, given of course the many reiterations of threats and warnings to keep silent that were given to her and everyone else who was there that night or subsequently involved to any real degree for that matter. She was specifically told by very high ranking military and government officials not to ever mention, to anyone, what she had been made privy to that night. However and despite all of that, Miriam somewhat couldn't help herself and ended up sharing the information she had with several members of her family. Of course, she in turn warned the people she told that they should never tell anyone what she had told them but you know how that goes and someone, somewhere and at some time, was bound to let something so big slip. The Roswell incident ended up dominating Miriam's life, and she started to really go off the rails because of it. She felt so paranoid and outside of herself it's said she entered into a loveless marriage and by the end of it all she had become a full blown alcoholic. It's understandable if you really think about it. Imagine that Roswell is real, because it is. Imagine that it really did happen as most of us in this community already know, and knowing about it way back then but not being able to discuss it for the fear of losing your life but then you can't keep it in anymore and you discuss it anyway and tell your family and those in your life you love the most and that are closest to you, only to worry then about them dying or being killed. And all of that only because of what you told them. It sounds like a lot, and for some, like Miriam, it sounds like it was way too much.

Miriam's life came to a shocking, and very suspicious end in the 1980s. Sometime in December of 1989, without telling anyone where she was going or why and with no one who knew her best knowing she had any plans to do so, she took off for a trip to San Jose, California where she checked into a motel under her sister's name. It was very out of character for her and her loved ones thought it was really bizarre behavior. Just her simply checking into the motel in general, even before what came next, was highly suspicious to her family. Many people familiar with the case believe that Miriam really was concerned she was being watched and was more than likely concerned her family was in danger and that maybe she was trying to put some distance between herself and the people she told about Roswell. After all, if she had nothing to hide and was merely just trying to get away from the stresses and pressures of daily life, why wouldn't she just use her own identification and her own name? The day after she checked in, motel staff went into her room and found Miriam dead, with a plastic bag tied tightly around her neck, with the bag portion over her face, obstructing her ability to breathe normally. She suffocated to death! There were very visible and clear marks on her arms that the staff member who checked her in said they hadn't noticed and that they definitely would've, when she checked in. The authorities said the marks were definitive indicators that a struggle and a scuffle had occurred sometime after she had checked in and more than likely while the bag was being placed around her face and tied to her neck. Despite ample evidence that she had been murdered, including the conclusions drawn by the authorities that I just shared with you all here, the official cause of death listed on Miriam's death certificate is that she took her own life. How about that?!

CHAPTER 37
PAUL PARADA

One of the strangest encounters I've come across in a very long time is also one of the most well known, at least in recent years, because it happened in 2019. Our witness is a paramedic who was responding to wildfires in the Amazon, and who found himself facing off with a ten foot tall humanoid creature unlike anything he had ever seen or experienced before. I've come across the researcher and documenter Albert Rosales many times before in my research and I respect his work greatly, which is why I have no qualms including an encounter directly from one of his personal files here. Rosales is somewhat well known for investigating these types of cases and bringing them into the view of the wider public. For obvious reasons, I can respect that.

On September 30, 2019 Paul Parada was working as a volunteer paramedic in the Bolivian region of the Amazon. At around eleven o'clock that night he stepped outside of the medical tent in order to smoke a cigarette but when he got out there he immediately noticed something strange a little off into the distance, seeming to be coming towards him as he stood there. It was too dark for Paul to really make out what it was he was looking at and possibly about to be confronted with, but he could see that it was very tall and had a humanoid shape to it. In fact, he later said the first thing he really noticed about the strange figure was how tall it was. As it continued to move closer to him, he also started to see more of what it looked like. He noticed its pale white skin and the fact that it was wearing a very shiny, almost metallic looking, one piece suit with several silver stripes on it. The strange and bizarre looking figure had long, shiny blonde hair that went down to a little below its shoulders. By the time Paul had taken all of that information in, the figure was within just feet of him, and he saw that whatever had approached him was pressing a towel or some other small piece of cloth/fabric up against its waist. It looked like it was injured and trying to apply pressure to the wound in order to stop the bleeding. Paul couldn't tell yet what he was looking at but with how close it was at that point, being mere feet from him, he saw it looked enough like a human man that his instincts kicked in and without moving towards it in any way, he called out and asked if the person needed assistance. The figure, whom Paul now really did think was a normal person who was, maybe not so normal- sort of like whoever it was, they were just an odd human being, replied to him in perfect Spanish. The figure said that he was injured and needed Paul's help. Paul immediately turned and went back into the medical tent to get some supplies and the figure followed closely behind him.

Paul later said that he'd had an inkling that something might be off with this person but a person is what he thought he was dealing with, despite all of the other strange things about it. In reality, what human being is ten feet tall? But, especially given what Paul was doing out there in the first place, it's like his brain did everything it could to reconcile itself to the fact that someone needed help and Paul could possibly provide it, leaving out all the other strange little details that made it so this couldn't possibly be a human being that he was dealing with. Paul got into the tent and started looking through his supplies, and then he turned around and asked the person what the issue was, probably so he knew what he would need to provide the best assistance possible. Without saying a word to him, the man removed the towels or whatever they were and Paul could immediately see that there was a gaping wound in the abdominal area. He began to treat the injury as soon as he saw it, without any hesitation. As he did so though he was fascinated and a bit taken back by the fact that despite all the blood gushing out from whatever the wound was, the man's clothes were completely unstained as though not a drop of blood had touched them, somehow. It was as though the clothing was made of some sort of waterproof material or something. While treating the injury he asked the guy how he had gotten injured in the first place, and his answer came telepathically, which obviously flabbergasted Paul. The man had spoken directly into our witness's mind and told him he had been attacked by a puma while walking through the forest. It must've been evident by the look on his face that Paul was terrified because the figure then told him, telepathically again, that he had nothing to worry about or fear and that no harm was meant towards him at all. Paul wasn't all that comforted by this but he did his best to maintain his composure and continued helping the figure by treating the wound. Just as he thought things couldn't get any more bizarre, Paul was proven wrong as the night took an even stranger turn soon after.

Paul finished treating the man's wound and when he was done, the man immediately got up to leave. He thanked Paul for his help but before he left, he asked him if he would go outside with him for a moment. Paul stood up and started to follow the strange man outside. As they were leaving the tent the figure spoke into Paul's mind again, saying, "you should not be shocked by what you are about to see." Paul I'm sure at this point was doing his best to keep his composure and who really knows how he was feeling at that moment but he followed the figure outside and that's when he saw a large, metallic and disc shaped object hovering several feet away from the tent and only a few feet from the ground. As he stared in awe at the object he also saw two humanoid figures inside of it. The humanoids were almost completely identical to the one he had just treated but instead of the pale white skin, these ones had green skin. The green humanoids didn't move the same way as the one he had just helped either. They had a mechanical movement to them, almost robotic, and this struck me as very interesting because in researching for this book and for the dozens of videos I've done about encounters with extraterrestrials on my channel, I've found that many times when people come across strange and somewhat mechanical entities that we and they think are more than likely extraterrestrials, they will often have a mechanical type of move- ment to them. Sometimes they even have robotic features. Paul didn't have much more of a reaction than shock and awe while looking at the green figures but he started to realize that if he stared for too long at them, he became overwhelmed with an intense sense of dread and fear. After a couple of minutes, the green figures- who had already exited and were somewhat wandering around underneath the craft at that point- started making their way in the direction of the entity Paul had just helped. Paul was standing next to that entity and so they were making their way towards him too. However, the taller and pale skinned humanoid then started to walk towards them, so that they would essentially be meeting in the middle and the green ones wouldn't get much closer to Paul. Paul just stood still watching the whole thing happen. The tall pale entity stopped and turned to look at Paul and shockingly, addressed him by his name. Paul hadn't told the entity his name at all, and he knew that it hadn't come up. He said later on that it actually startled him a little more than probably everything else that was going on in some odd way. Maybe there's something so personal about a name that it would be almost terrifying for some out of this world creature to address us in that way and by all accounts that's how Paul felt too. The weird part of this is that it seems like the story is a bit incomplete and I wonder if it's because Paul doesn't remember what was said. The tall pale humanoid turned to face him and said his name, and then the next thing Paul remembers is turning and walking back into the medical tent. Paul's mind was reeling but he didn't stick around outside for long enough to see the humanoids and the craft leave. I feel like this was compulsion at play but who knows?

Aside from discussing the incident with his brother, who was also in that same region and also volunteering his own medical skills, Paul really didn't talk about what happened to him that night with anyone. Not at first, anyway. Over the course of the next few months Paul couldn't stop thinking about what he had experienced and it was legitimately starting to drive him crazy. He would suffer through extreme bouts of insomnia and when he did sleep the dreams were scary and intense, almost like lucid dreaming but a little bit different. Eventually he decided he needed to talk more about what happened to him that night in order to try and work through and possibly even heal from it. At the very least he figured talking about it would help him come to terms with it, if nothing else. Oddly enough too, Paul had saved the towel/fabric thing the entity had initially been holding against its wounds in order to stop the blood from gushing but as of right now and for frustratingly unknown reasons, no DNA tests have ever been conducted on that material- as far as the general public knows about anyway. What the figure was, what it was doing there, where it came from etc are all great questions and all still have absolutely no real answers. As with almost everything else in this community and regarding these types of experiences, it's all left to the public to theorize and speculate, never gaining the satisfaction of knowing if we're right or wrong about any of it.

I wholeheartedly believe that DNA and other important tests were run on that fabric and the government knows exactly what those creatures were and the answers to all of the above mentioned questions and more but they're never going to tell the general public about it. A person is smart but people in groups tend to panic and all sorts of horrible things happen when scared people get together and react to something, so I doubt we will ever really know the answers to this one, at least not anytime soon. Another thing I was thinking about as I went through and researched this encounter was how the description of the tall, pale humanoid entity that Paul had initially come across and eventually ended up helping is extremely similar in nature to the abundance of humanoid encounters that came to light in the 1950s from all over the world. Before researching into this I thought the most popular extraterrestrial entity as far as visitations go at that time, meaning in the 1950s and 60s, were the alien grays as we've come to call them and that's true for certain areas of the world and also it's true as far as abductions were concerned, but these so-called "Nordic" aliens have also been spotted and encountered just as much, if not more, at that time in history. Nordics are typically very friendly and not aggressive at all, and it seems as though they would visit with certain humans to increase the knowledge of the person or people encountering them. They also seemingly liked to be of assistance in offering spiritual guidance to those humans as well. One very important point I want to touch on is that most of the encounters with these Nordic entities are not abductions but simple interactions and encounters and usually the human or humans involved don't leave physically harmed, even if they inadvertently become psychologically and/or emotionally damaged a little bit due to the experience, as Paul had. The respective witnesses always remained with the entities out of their own free will and weren't forced in any way into the encounters.

Some researchers and others who have come across these types of encounters wonder if the Nordic beings could possibly be connected to the angelic beings we often come across in the Bible. If that's the case then it's possible that the so-called "angels" in the Bible are actually some sort of extraterrestrial beings, made of flesh and blood, and who knows what else? Could that be the case? Only with them being a lot more like humans than we initially thought? After all, the being in Paul's encounter was bleeding, even if in a very bizarre way where his clothes weren't getting wet from it, and supernatural beings and entities don't bleed. At the end of the day though there's obviously no way of knowing and it's a huge and extremely fascinating mystery. At least in my opinion, even as someone who knows angels exist and that they're completely and totally spiritual beings. It's still an odd connection and I wonder what to make of it.

CHAPTER 38
TALL WHITES

On the afternoon of July 6, 2009 in Wiltshire, England, an off-duty police sergeant was driving along some of the country back roads in the area and minding his own business, when he saw something odd over to the side of the road in one of the many large fields that surrounded it. He slowed down and turned to look in that direction and saw a bunch of what he described as "strange looking men" walking around. They were wandering aimlessly as far as he could tell, in one of the cornfields. At first he thought that it was most likely just some teenagers hanging out and not bothering anyone but possibly sneaking some beers or something in the cornfield. However, for reasons he couldn't explain, he said a "strange feeling" came over him almost immediately upon setting eyes on the men. He decided to pull over and investigate the situation further. As he got out of the car and started to cross the field, making his way towards the cornfield, he said the so-called "strange feeling" was becoming increasingly stronger with each step he took. As he got even closer, he noticed that each of the men was at least six feet tall, possibly even taller. They were all dressed in what looked like white overalls and they were all staring down and moving around as though they were looking for something on the ground. The officer dismissed the idea that these were just some teenagers trying to sneak some alcohol and started thinking of other reasons why these men would be there, doing what they were doing and dressed as they were. He thought maybe they were some sort of forensics team or something like that. He thought that based on how they seemingly were looking for something and how they were dressed. With that thought he considered that a major crime had possibly been committed and because it was his job to do so, he started walking more confidently and much more quickly up to the men in order to ask if he could be of any assistance. As he got even closer still though, he started to hear what sounded like crackling "static electricity" all around him. He stopped and listened and realized that the strange and out of place buzzing noise sounded like it was constantly moving all around him and with each crackle and pop, the ears of corn would move in the exact spot where it sounded like the static was coming from. It was bizarre to say the least.

Realizing something very strange was going on and not sure of what to do next, our witness decided to call out to the men instead of continuing to approach them. He yelled out and asked if they needed any assistance, announced himself and his job title and asked what they were all doing out there. However, none of the men even looked up, let alone in his direction. It was almost like they hadn't even heard him at all, which was impossible given how loud he yelled and how close he was to them at that point. After they ignored him for a minute or two and with him just standing there wondering what to do next and what he had gotten himself into, they all suddenly and in perfect unison stopped what they were doing and looked up. Our witness said it was like they all suddenly became aware of his presence all at once, all at the same time. After stopping for a split second, all of the men, which our witness now counted as three of them, started running "faster than any man" he had ever seen. Within a second or two they'd all disappeared into thin air right before his eyes! The static/crackling sound was still very much present and the ears of corn continued to move all around him with each little popping sound. For the first time since all of this started, our witness said the "strange feeling" turned into outright terror and he turned and ran for his life, fleeing the odd scene as fast as his legs could carry him back to his vehicle. He had to sit in his car for a few moments and collect himself before continuing on with his day, and as he was doing that, about two or three minutes after he initially entered the car again, he started it up and made his way home. By the time he got to his house he had a migraine headache accompanied by such extreme nausea that he almost went to the hospital. Instead he rested and it seems like it went away eventually on its own.

Later that same evening he decided to report the experience to his superior officer, despite how insane he knew it sounded, but his superior refused to investigate the incident any further. There isn't any official report of this on record because our witness wasn't on duty at the time but he was told by that same superior officer and others whom he confided in to "just forget about it and move on from it." However, because of how bizarre and surreal the whole encounter/experience was for our witness, he couldn't stop thinking about and analyzing every single detail of what he'd witnessed that day. He started digging up information about the area, just trying to make sense of it all, or at least a little bit, but instead what he found further confused him. In that same area where he'd had his encounter, he saw that a crop circle had recently sprung up, at the exact same time he had witnessed all of this. Once he was able to verify that a crop circle had in fact randomly sprung up in the same exact field where he had encountered those men and either on that same day or a day or two later- my sources weren't clear- he contacted a researcher and expert local to him, whose name was Andrew Russell.

Andrew Russell looked into the incident and very quickly determined that our witness had in fact come across a trio of so-called "tall white" extraterrestrials. Russell was unsure whether the aliens had created the crop circle or if they were there investigating it themselves. I wonder though, if you think back to the incident I just recounted for you, you'll remember the static electricity sounds he kept hearing all around him and the fact it seemed to our witness as though the corn were reacting in some way to whatever those noises were. For me, that feels like he was standing there in the middle of that cornfield as the crop circle was forming. The snap, crackle and pop noises could have been the crop circle springing to life, at least in my opinion, so while the tall whites being there to investigate the circle itself makes some sense, due to those additional details, it's more likely for me that they were in the middle of forming it when our witness came upon them. Before we move on I want to call your attention to something I come across a lot when researching these types of seemingly random and bizarre encounters with extraterrestrials and that's the fact that the three entities our sergeant saw were all looking down at the ground, as though they were collecting data or were otherwise on some sort of strange fact finding mission. I've often come across people coming running into alien forms in the woods and other places who were collecting samples of the soil or water in the area, and that's why I wasn't as surprised when I read through this encounter. I don't know what the answers are, but it all seems to be connected somehow, at least from all the research I've done into these types of things.

CHAPTER 39
THE BRIDGE

In the early morning hours of August 11, 2003 at just a little after four o'clock another encounter involving humanoid entities happened. This time it took place just outside of Szczecinek, Poland. This one comes from the files of Biran Vike, and he obtained the information from a Polish UFO investigator named Tomek Wierszalowic. According to the report, a man named Lech Chacinski was driving himself to work along some back country roads, as he had done every day he'd gone to work for years. He was in his work truck and approached a bridge he had driven over many times before. Everything was perfectly normal and usual, until it wasn't. As he approached the bridge in his truck, a humanoid figure suddenly appeared in the middle of the road not too far up ahead of him. He focused on the strange looking and out of place figure, trying to determine what it was and what it could have possibly been doing there at that time in the early morning. The figure was standing there facing his truck with its hand out in a greeting gesture and as he stared at it, Lech also noticed that two other identical figures were standing right behind that one, flanking it on either side. He pulled his truck to the side of the road and turned the engine off, all the while examining what he was looking at and trying to wrap his mind around whatever it was. He saw that each figure was wearing a shiny suit, which he thought looked very similar to the suits astronauts wear here on Earth. More concerningly though, our witness said he couldn't escape the deepening feeling growing within him that he was witnessing something "disturbingly extraordinary." Despite appearing human in almost every conceivable way, he knew this was something spectacular that he was seeing, and he couldn't take his eyes off of the three figures. He said they had two arms, two legs, stood bipedally, were all of average height etc. He further described their clothing and said that the suits were shiny, but with the appearance of "dull, silvery, elastic foil that looked puffed out." Each figure also wore a large helmet with a large black visor that covered where their face would have other-wise been visible. He said that there were "seven lights in each row" on their torsos, and the lights flashed all different colors. On their backs, each figure carried some kind of backpack, which some believe could have actually been some sort of breathing apparatus, by the way it was later described by our witness.

Before he even had time to blink, our witness said one of the figures was outside of his truck's cabin and peeking through one of the side windows. Because of how close the entity now was, he could somewhat see its face a lot better underneath the large black visor on the helmet. He said he could easily make out "two round black eyes" staring directly at him. He was so scared and unnerved by the intensity and look of the eyes glaring at him, that he immediately tried to start his truck up so he could get the hell out of there as quickly as humanly possible. Before he could do so though, "a beam of light" came shooting out of the creature's helmet and it hit him. He blacked out immediately. He came to a few minutes later, not understanding what had just happened to him but with an extreme sense of calm washing over him. He also heard a voice at that time, inside of his head, and he somehow just knew it was the creature speaking to him telepathically. The voice told him he shouldn't be afraid and it asked as well if he could hear them. Without understanding how he did so, our witness said he was surprised when he was able to telepathically communicate back to them, telling them that he could indeed hear them but not with his ears. The figure then started to ask him questions about his truck. It asked "what material" it was made out of and what type of fuel it used. He answered their questions with his mind and said the look of "great surprise and wonder" on the creature's face at his responses struck him as unusual. After they discussed the vehicle, the creature almost casually just started telling our witness about the "catastrophic consequences" awaiting our planet if human beings didn't change and if we were to continue on our current course. Our witness can't recall anything more specific that was said but knows a whole conversation had taken place. One thing he definitely remembered was asking the creature where it was from and the response it gave him. The creature told him, "the eighth galaxy is our home." I had to look this up and if the internet is correct then there actually is a place scientists have found that we call the eighth galaxy. Here's a tiny snippet of what I found. "The eighth galaxy is ESO 444-46, which is the eighth largest known galaxy in the universe. It's classified as a supergiant elliptical galaxy and is believed to have grown to its current size by merging with and absorbing other galaxies." I looked up whether or not there's known intelligent life on the eighth galaxy and got the answer that, "researchers and scientists have calculated that there could be more than thirty intelligent civilizations throughout our galaxy. While direct evidence for alien life is lacking, the commonness of habitable environments in the universe suggests that such life forms may exist." So, I was given a typical and very disappointing non-answer. Thanks Google!

Back to our witness in Poland. He said he has no clue how long the conversation lasted but when it was over all three of the humanoid figures just floated up into the air and away from the road, and they went into a disc shaped craft that had been hovering nearby. He didn't know if the metallic craft had just arrived or if it had been there the whole time, waiting somewhere nearby throughout the entire encounter. He described it as being at least one hundred feet wide and floating approximately one thousand feet from where he had pulled over and parked his truck. He saw several rows of windows running alongside the upper part of the object, while in the center of the very top, there was an "opaque chamber." He watched as the three figures positioned themselves directly below the craft and without warning, a "very bright blue-white light" came from underneath it and "took the three beings up" into the object. Within a minute the figures and the craft were gone. All that remained of it was "colored smoke" which our witness said had also wrapped itself all around the craft as it was taking off into the sky. He watched on in awe as the craft rose into the air, to an altitude of between one hundred and one hundred and fifty feet before slowly moving across the ground, with the smoke following it the whole time and continuing to swirl around it. It briefly stopped for no more than a second or two and then shot up into the morning sky. The sound it made was also very strange and, according to our witness, sounded like a cross between buzzing and hissing. He was amazed when he looked to where the craft had been hovering just seconds earlier and saw clear indentations in the crops that made a perfect outline of the spaceship itself. He took several pictures of those marks in the field, and later on during subsequent investigations into his report, even more photos of those same indentations were captured. Many UFO investigators looked into this encounter and ended up going into the field to see if they could gather additional evidence over the years and most of them believe this encounter happened and that Lech is an honest and very credible witness, with no reason to lie and nothing he was trying to gain from talking about his bizarre and fascinating encounter.

CHAPTER 40
THE RIVER WEAVER SIGHTING

Now we are going to move on to an encounter that in my opinion is one of the most insane and thought provoking that I've ever come across, and many people agree with me on that one. It happened on the evening of January 27, 1978 along the banks of the River Weaver in Cheshire, England. I found an article that gives details of the encounter and that has the witness statements in Volume 26, Number 3, 1980 Edition of the Flying Saucer Review by Paul Whetnall and Jenny Randles. At around six o'clock that night four young men were out poaching pheasants near the river in an area that had come to be known by locals as The Devil's Garden. And this location, whether by coincidence or happenstance or whatever else, has a lot of strange legends attached to it along with people who have had many different types of strange experiences there. Because they were out committing a crime at the time of their encounter, none of the four men would allow their real names to be used publicly and they all insisted on anonymity throughout all of it. They are still just a group of four anonymous men today. As they looked for the pheasants all around the riverbank and in the woods surrounding it, one of the men suddenly saw what he described as "a strange object" that looked like it was kind of skimming all along the surface of the water. Now, you have to keep in mind that at this time there had been widespread news reports about a Soviet satellite that had come crashing down onto the ground in Canada, and so it makes sense that when he called his friend's attention to the object on the water, they all initially thought that they were looking at another satellite falling to Earth, regardless of where they might've thought it had originally come from. They watched the object for a few minutes and as they did they started to realize that they were witnessing something extraordinary and possibly more out of this world than any satellite sent into outer space by the Cold War superpowers here on earth. They quickly realized that it wasn't falling and had to have been under some sort of intelligent control, as it was moving across the water and hovering above the ground, about twenty feet high, on top of the woodlands.

As it passed directly over the four men, they heard what they later described as "a light humming sound" that appeared to be coming from it. Also as it passed directly over their heads, they said "a strange wind" also seemed to follow after it. They all said that the "wind" made them feel fairly sick to their stomachs too. From where it flew above them around twenty feet over their heads, they could clearly see it better than they had when it had been over the water and the woods, and they all described it in the same way later on. It was spherical and had a silver exterior, and they watched in shock as it descended to the ground and landed very near where they were standing. They later said that the object had been approximately fifteen feet long across, and had multiple lines of flashing lights all around the sides of it. They saw several areas that looked like they could have been windows, and they said "a very strange glow" could be seen emanating from within the craft. The men said that they could only look for so long at the craft itself, for a minute or two at a time, before they felt forced to turn away because their eyes started to burn so badly. UFO researchers would later confirm that this had been some sort of ultraviolet light, which as many of you know our human eyes are not supposed to be looking at. The more they looked at it, looked away and then looked back again, the more "fuzzy looking" the craft became to them. The "fuzziness" made them feel like there could be potential radiation or something of that nature all around the craft, and they were more and more concerned the longer they all stood there but I'm sure that wasn't enough for them to go running away through the woods because if you think about it, at that point, what really do you do in that type of situation? Most people seem to agree that their curiosity would more than likely overpower their instinct to turn and run away.

So anyway, they did begin to back away from the object eventually, very slowly, in light of the possibility that they were being exposed to radiation poisoning. Before they could turn around and even try to slowly and somehow make their way out of there, they noticed a humanoid figure coming out of the object. It was wearing a one piece silver suit, somewhat metallic looking, and it had a large round helmet on its head. On top of the helmet there was a violet light. The four witnesses stood as still as possible, probably thinking they didn't want to make any sudden moves or draw any extra attention to themselves in light of how bizarre and terrifying the situation had suddenly become. It seemed as though the humanoid figure was looking around the area and using the light on top of its helmet to do so. The violet light swung its beam all around the area, eventually stopping on a herd of cows in a nearby field. After a minute or two the figure turned and got back into the craft but the men still didn't want to risk drawing any attention to themselves and so they still didn't move. They were right, too, because just a few moments later the figure re-emerged from the craft but this time it had an identical looking humanoid figure following behind it. They were carrying something between them and it looked to the men like it was a large, silver, metal cage. It looked like it was very light because of the ease with which the two figures seemed to be able to carry and handle the cage. The figures started in the direction of where that herd of cows were grazing.

The two figures approached one of the cows grazing there in that field, and this cow was with the herd but more off to the side than any of the others. It was basically standing alone and the figures immediately went up to it with the cage still between them. It was very clear to the four anonymous men watching that something was different about that cow and it dawned on them that it seemed to be standing there unnaturally still, not moving or even, seemingly at least, breathing or grazing at all like the others. It looked like it had been unnaturally frozen or something, frozen to the spot it stood in, as if it had been paralyzed while standing up! The figures placed the cage around the cow and then began to slide some metal disks into place on it. The witnesses began to wonder to themselves if the figures were planning on taking the cow with them back inside their ship or if they were merely doing something like weighing and measuring it. They didn't stay to find out, unfortunately for us and this really did frustrate me a bit when I first read it. Instead of waiting to see what happened next, all four of the men finally turned and ran away from the bizarre and terrifying scene as fast as they could. They eventually made their way to a bridge that allowed them to cross to the other side of the river and they got the hell out of there quickly. They did turn once and look back in the direction from which they'd just come but they were unable to see either the humanoids or their craft. One of the witnesses told investigators that he had experienced a strange sort of "pulling sensation" as he fled the scene, as if there had been some sort of "invisible force" trying to drag him back. What made this even more bizarre is that he said that the force had been trying to pull him back by his testicles, of all things. He stated his testicles were sore for several days after the encounter. It's been almost a half a century and still we have no explanation for what these four men witnessed out there that night.

My initial reaction to this encounter was that perhaps they were watching the beginnings of what we've come to know in this community as the cattle mutilations, many of which have taken place in England. However, I looked into this theory of mine and found that there had been no reports of dead or missing cattle in that area in the days following the men's encounter. Could this have been another sort of intelligence gathering mission? Like the ones where we always see extraterrestrial creatures gathering soil, water and even sometimes air samples? Could it be that the cow was taken but that it was returned, seemingly unharmed and unchanged, before anyone had the chance to notice it was gone? Did they do something else altogether but in the field there so that they didn't have to take or harm the animal? These are great questions but none have answers and no one knows still to this day what those men witnessed out there. What we do know, what I did uncover, is that these types of sightings became common in that area at that time. What was their business with that cow?

Just four weeks before the River Weaver encounter we just discussed, on January 2, 1978, someone living in Rainford, in the Merseyside region of northwestern England reported seeing a humanoid figure wearing a silver suit. Just a little over two weeks later, on January 18 and in that same region, several school children said that they had all seen "a small UFO" land on the roof of their school. The kids said that, to their great astonishment, right after the "small UFO" landed on the roof, they watched as three "astronauts" got out of the craft and walked around the top of the building. They said the "astronauts" were wearing shiny suits that looked golden in color. I wonder though, as do many others, if the suits were in fact silver but were reflecting the sun and therefore looked like they were golden instead. Do you think these other sightings are connected to the River Weaver incident with the four anonymous poachers? I don't know but I wouldn't label it as a coincidence, that's for sure. I want to make it known here too that there was a discreet wave of UFO sightings happening in the UK at this exact time, and that several people said they'd also been abducted, having eventually come forward with their stories. Because of everything I just mentioned, it seems as though the River Weaver sighting, as it's come to be called, had taken on even greater interest and significance with UFOlogists and other researchers from all over the world. It's still widely discussed and argued over today.

AFTERWORD

GEMMA JADE

While it's true my first love in this community of the unknown is the paranormal, with true crime being a close second, I have been covering a lot of material on extraterrestrials lately as well, and doing a lot of research into it. It goes beyond the videos I put out on my YouTube channel and even my own personal experiences because I am looking for actual proof, tangible evidence that no one could ever deny. However, the conclusion I've drawn is that it doesn't matter what type of evidence is presented and no matter how obvious it is that aliens have visited us, do abduct us and do exist, if someone wants to cover that up and deny it, if they're powerful enough, they will. I feel sometimes like I'm being led to something so much bigger than I could possibly imagine or wrap my mind around. This might be because I've uncovered bits and pieces of repressed memories of abductions and healings I've personally experienced, that I've never remembered or knew anything about before. As I took the time to write this book, all of those experiences seemingly intensified in my mind because I keep receiving tiny clips, just for a millisecond, of conversations and visitations- contact I've made with all sorts of otherworldly beings during sleep. I can't explain it very well yet and it's nothing more than little scraps of information and memory right now, which is why I've only gone over one encounter in this book that I've had personally. However, I do plan on making this a series, so I will continue to add more as I regain more of the memories and information. Like anyone else who believes that they're uncovering repressed or screened memories and not just thinking up crazy scenarios on their own, I find it scary and confusing. When I am ready, I will put it all out there, uncensored.

I wasn't really sure what to name this book because I've gone through and covered so many different experiences where people have encountered some sort of strange and bizarre humanoid beings or entities on my channel and I've been covering these types of things for years. That's what makes it all the more believable to me though, is the fact that I must have gone through and gone over at least five hundred or more different types of encounters with all different types of creatures and beings, throughout the ages and all cultures and yet each and every day more people are still coming forward with more sightings and encounters with them. Not to mention, it seems as though every single day as well, someone encounters something completely unknown that no one has ever encountered before. A lot of the time the sightings are one offs and every once in a while there will also be some interaction between the witness and the beings but more often than not, despite falling somewhat under a similar title, these encounters are so incredibly different that it's somewhat hard to be able to classify which ones should go into which book. It isn't stopping or even slowing down anytime soon, is my point. That's why it doesn't matter to me how many of these books I need to write or how many videos I need to do, as long as I am bringing you all accurate information to the best of my ability and showing you all how incredibly and terrifyingly in some cases, these types of encounters are.

I often wonder if these different types of humanoid creatures are all coming from other places or if they're residing a lot closer to home than most of us would ever dare to think- or want to know.

In fact, it hasn't escaped my attention that encounters like the ones I've covered in this book go back as far as civilization or even time itself, and it's these types of encounters and witness statements that are actually the basis for a great deal of the myths and legends we are all so very familiar with today, in all areas of the supernatural and paranormal realms. Also, and as I've talked about somewhat at length in my first book Missing: The Fae Theory, it's where we've gotten a lot of our modern day fairytales from; from the somewhat obscure to the very well known, this is where they come from. It seems to me as though the age of UFOs came into being right around the same time that the modern day UFO era began, which was sometime in the 1940s. The fact that millions or more of these bizarre and terrifying encounters are all on record, makes them all the more believable for me and so many others. Records usually exist when there's been research put into what's being recorded and that includes witness statements and any and all other evidence that doesn't go to contradict what the person or people in question say happened or is happening to them. In my opinion it would be impossible to document each and every time someone had an encounter with something from another world or dimension, since the beginning of time. All I can do is present to you the information I have, and if you're new to my work then please know, I never repeat anything I do not believe. Meaning, if I bring you a disappearance that I believe is supernatural in nature, or an encounter someone had with some sort of creature from another dimension or extraterrestrial being, it is because I wholeheartedly believe that encounter really happened. I hope you enjoyed this book and I look forward to writing the sequel and seeing what other insanely terrifying and mind-bending encounters I come across when I'm writing it. Thank you.

ABOUT THE AUTHOR

Gemma Jade, a spiritual medium from Paterson, New Jersey, has spent her life exploring the vast realms of the supernatural, paranormal, and extraterrestrial. Her profound experiences have fueled her passion, leading her to author several acclaimed books. Among her works is an Amazon best-selling exploration of the Black Eyed Kids phenomenon, offering mind-expanding theories about these mysterious beings, and a deep dive into shadow entities that transcends the common understanding of sleep paralysis.

On her YouTube channel, *Gemma Jade*, she captivates her audience with enthralling discussions on all things paranormal and metaphysical. Her live streams, oracle readings, and spiritual insights provide a sanctuary for those seeking knowledge and guidance in the mystical arts.

A gifted spiritual healer and teacher, Gemma is dedicated to helping others navigate their spiritual journeys. She is always accessible for inquiries and support at GemmaJadeParanormal@gmail.com. Join Gemma Jade in her extraordinary journey through the unknown, where every encounter is an invitation to explore the mysteries of the universe.

ALSO BY GEMMA JADE

Missing: The Fae Theory

Gone: Mysterious Disappearances

Campfire Stories: Encounters in the Woods

Midnight Visitors: True Stories of Black-Eyed Kids

Danger at Your Door: Encounters with Black Eyed Kids

Encounters with Evil

Shadow Entities: Sleep Paralysis and Beyond

www.ingramcontent.com/pod-product-compliance
Lightning Source LLC
Chambersburg PA
CBHW021137260726

48656CB00023B/168